Series / Number 01-046

Political Man:
Toward a Conceptual Base

RUTH LANE
The American University

⑤ SAGE PUBLICATIONS / Beverly Hills / London

For information address:

SAGE PUBLICATIONS, INC.
275 South Beverly Drive
Beverly Hills, California 90212

SAGE PUBLICATIONS LTD
St George's House / 44 Hatton Garden
London EC1N 8ER

International Standard Book Number 0-8039-0308-1

Library of Congress Catalog Card No. 73-87845

FIRST PRINTING

When citing a professional paper, please use the proper form. Remember to cite the
correct Sage Professional Paper series title and include the paper number. One of the
two following formats can be adapted (depending on the style manual used):

(1) NAMENWIRTH, J. Z. and LASSWELL, H. D. (1970) "The Changing Language of
American Values." Sage Professional Papers in Comparative Politics, 1, 01-001.
Beverly Hills and London: Sage Pubns.

OR

(2) Namenwirth, J. Zvi and Lasswell, Harold D. 1970. *The Changing Language of
American Values.* Sage Professional Papers in Comparative Politics, vol. 1, series no.
01-001. Beverly Hills and London: Sage Publications.

CONTENTS

Political Man:
Toward a Conceptual Base

RUTH LANE
The American University

I. POLITICAL MAN

Citizens, we shall say to them in our tale, you are brothers, yet God has framed you differently. Some of you have the power of command, and in the composition of these he has mingled gold, wherefore also they have the greatest honor; others he has made of silver, to be auxiliaries; others again who are to be husbandmen and craftsmen he has composed of brass and iron . . . And God proclaims as a first principle to the rulers, and above all else, that there is nothing which they should so anxiously guard, or of which they are to be such good guardians, as of the purity of the race. . . . For an oracle says that when a man of brass or iron guards the state, it will be destroyed.
—Plato, *The Republic,* Book III
(Jowett, 1942: 303-304).

THE BACKGROUND

That political science has been concerned with the problem of political man and his definition for over 2,300 years is perhaps a dismal note to sound at the beginning of another such study. Yet Plato was clearly correct in his appreciation of the scientific problem faced by students of the political system: Unless informed by psychological insights, the study of "government" is but an exercise in history and rhetoric.[1] This is so, not for indefinable, "normative" reasons, but because political science as a nomothetic inquiry and the practice of government as its architectonic branch must have a basis in empirical fact. And the logic of the inquiry, as Plato knew and as "behavioralism" rediscovered, must force the political scientist ever closer to the basic political fact of "man."[2]

Yet it would seem that the discipline of political science only variably recognizes the need for a science of man, and rather prefers to build its hypotheses on more "abstract" foundations.[3] As prelude to the present "model of man," we would argue that building science on such abstractions is almost inevitably to fall into the parochial error of unconsciously building on one's own biasses, in lieu of conscious theory.[4] And the parochial error is an error because it leads its followers into advocating policies that don't work, reforms that miss the mark, improvements that have no noticeable effect, "development" that more resembles disaster, and perhaps least publically dangerous of all, it leads to "science" that lacks any capacity to explain, or even to predict events.[5]

Analytically, the point may be seen with great clarity through Alker's (1965: 29-34) neo-Aristotelian model of "justice." Justice occurs, in the model definition, when $v_i = e_i$: when the value received by each individual in the relevant group is equivalent to that individual's expectations about what he ought to get.[6] Taking a wide perspective on a model designed admittedly for more narrow ends allows the formulation of a political research problem that has implications in almost every subfield of political science: What are, in fact, the "expectations" of the individuals being studied? That the expectations of other segments of mankind are not necessarily those of political scientists, and that we cannot infer validly from our selves to theirs, should have become clear long ago; but we still tend to plug *our* expectations into *their* equations, and then wonder why the "solution" frequently is not what was expected.

The only way for political science to realistically orient its research and to fill in a solid theoretical foundation under its increasingly elegant models is to face up to the diversity of man and reattempt from the modern perspective what Plato attempted from his—the "measurement" of man. But we must avoid, at least at the outset, the idea that this measurement will be ordinal; for one can see in Plato the source of parochialism in political psychology—the unfortunate nomenclature of "gold," "silver," "brass," and "iron." However, if his basic premise is stripped to its most usable (and perhaps most accurate) form, it can become a starting point even for "democratic" political scientists.[7]

This postulate—that men differ—if accepted as a basis for scientific inquiry, allows for comprehension of the human variety found by students of comparative politics, without any necessary imposition of culturally focussed preferences. It opens the way to the basic scientific stance of "what sorts of people have we here?" rather than the perhaps more typical question, "why aren't those people . . . more like me?"

There may be an additional reluctance to undertake a systematic political psychology in the feeling that it is inherently radical, no matter what its particular content, and that in merely looking at the "roots" we may damage them by simple exposure, if nothing else. But the implications of failing to lay this psychological base for empirical work are a heavy counterweight to such "conservative" considerations. Caught between normative political philosophers who fight obsolescence in an era where philosophy has given way to linguistics and rugged empiricists whose sandhills of raw facts keep collapsing in the absence of theoretic shoring, comparative political science seems like the voice in the wilderness between, calling in vain for middle-range theory useful in its scientific concerns.[8]

To turn to the other social sciences for help is to discover that the problems are the same everywhere—speculative theory that fails to convince, empirical research that fails to converge.[9] Nor do the blessings of the division of labor seem to be occurring—the political scientist cannot simply use the output of the psychologist, or the sociologist; in practical effect, the questions in which he is interested are not being answered, at least in suitable form, elsewhere in the social sciences.

Our argument is not that political science can be shown to have some unique focus that gives it true identity in the face of encroaching social sciences; nor, certainly, that its concerns are entirely distinct from theirs. But there is a sense in which the adjective "political" simplifies its noun, whatever that noun be. The psychologist must study man in his full complexity; the political scientist can settle for less, quite a bit less if necessary. The sociologist, as he speculates on any two individuals in an interaction situation, must be somewhat intimidated by the range of possible outcomes; the political scientist, contemplating the same two abstract individuals, sees fewer interesting outcomes; perhaps he need ask only "who wins?" or "who governs?" The political scientist could be temporarily satisfied, according to this line of approach, with a theory of man that would allow him to describe the types of individuals that he comes across in his political concerns.

The history of political thought is a rich source with which to begin building such a theory of man, although one may be somewhat deterred by the tendency of political science to regard its theorists as saints to be revered rather than thinkers to be utilized in the conduct of inquiry. The more practical barrier may be the failure of the "great" theorists to build typologies, rather than balancing their whole arguments on the pivot of a single-factor theory that describes all men.

The paradigm to which political science has returned cyclically since the days of Thrasymachus is the most durable of these overgeneralizations, and its current reappearance as "economic man" again proves its utility.[10] The height to which one can build on a unidimensional base is, however, limited;[11] if the American political scientist can make do with this model, the researcher abroad is less fortunate. What is self-evident at home is anathema elsewhere. The requisite is plainly for a complementary psychological theory that will allow political science to deal with the variegated humanity it studies; and it must be one that helps him not to pass judgments, but to describe with some broad degree of accuracy.

This need not imply that political science should go off on another classical chase after truth, beauty, and the nature of man. The empiricist as well as the traditionalist may prefer to allow some mystery concerning such verities to remain untouched. But political science seems in little danger, ethically, of going too far in the study of man.[12] The danger is rather that of never insisting on an answer to the question, "What, if anything, have we learned concerning political man in the past 2,300 years?"

MODELLING MAN

It is perhaps only to complete skeptics or to "overconscious" thinkers that the problems involved in the building of a model of man from the ground up are obvious.[13] To develop such a formal model one must move somehow beyond the historically specific level—with all its implicit biasses—to the general, high-abstraction level, where true cross-cultural description is possible.[14] As usual, the context of comparative politics makes this most clear. In the various national settings with which the individual scientist works, it quickly appears that the "home truths" are insufficient; the saving clause of "ceteris paribus" no longer saves; and psychopolitical man rather than being the empirical base of our response becomes the "residual" explanatory agent.[15]

There are numerous possible responses to this uncertain if not confused situation: the search for ever-better data, the development of ever-more-powerful statistical techniques, or alternatively, the retreat into a rigorous historicism that considers all events as unique and ultimately precludes science. Another alternative, less often perceived in these days when political theorists are so frequently defined as "keepers of the flame," is the constructive development of theory· that can serve as a guide to research[16] by systematizing extant research findings and thus redirecting new research along paths that, while not necessarily fruitful, are at least consciously chosen.

Under this interpretation, the theoretic function is not a zero-sum game but an ongoing, critical, constructive feedback process. The theory involved is not intended to be true or false, but to be useful and falsifiable, perhaps simultaneously. Such theory serves as a map, capable of showing with slightly more than a worm's-eye view what the surrounding country looks like, where the unexplored areas are, and what the next stage of the journey most practicably might be. The map does not tell anyone where to go, but it does make possible decisions based on a broader, better-organized array of information.[17]

What the model will suggest is that properly viewed—from, as it were, a high enough hill—there is more coherence to our empirical studies than might have been thought. Political science tends to ask rather consistently certain types of questions concerning psychopolitical man; this is true whether one reads the Platonic dialogs or the *American Political Science Review* (although the language and premises may differ somewhat). How does man perceive himself? How does he view his world? How does he perceive his fellow human beings? What, in the long run as well as the short run, does he want? These questions may be summarized: (1) What is involved in man's political self-identity—in his definition of himself, his membership groups, his reference groups; and conversely in his "anti-self" groups—his enemies? and (2) What is involved in the making of political choices, at a degree of depth sufficient to be useful in many decision areas—elections, legislatures, administration, small groups, and games? [18]

Classical and modern political theorists and contemporary social scientists have provided a broad range of responses to these questions, but we do not have a framework sufficient to the variety of that response. Not to put too fine a face on it, we need a clothesline sufficient to the laundry we must hang out.[19] And somewhere, among the multifarious facets of the vocation of political theory, must be found this willingness to aid political science by going out on an epistemological limb and asking not "what is X?" but rather "what can be conveniently or profitably regarded as X?" (Rapoport, 1966; 1953). The model here to be discussed claims only to be an attempt in the tradition of the latter orientation.

Perhaps the greatest danger in this sort of endeavor is the possibility of the reification of one's own biasses, so that the resultant construct fails almost entirely of extension—its parameters fit nothing but the case for which it was designed. To limit this problem, the attempt has been to encompass as much as possible of the relatively "hard" empirical research available on the topic of political man. Since the American field has been the most extensively plowed in this area, the model may appear to be seriously biassed. Two integral aspects of the model may be seen as alleviating this problem.

(1) The dimensional nature of each module requires the analyst to consider an alternative polarity to his own perspective at least eleven times in applying the basic framework. While this may not avoid the fallacy of the excluded middle, it is some improvement on the use of a single pattern with only one negative alternative (e.g., "democratic" vs. "undemocratic").

(2) The model is sufficiently precise that it can be determined where it does and does not fit: it is testable in the sense of a scientific hypothesis, being—like any model—merely a coherent pattern of hypotheses. This means that when an investigator finds that a part (or the whole) does *not* fit, in the particular nation or group with which he is working, incremental action can be taken: if a part fails, it can be replaced because of the modular nature of the model; if the postulated modules are insufficient, more can be added; and if the whole model fails on wide empirical testing, then its elimination will mean that the next theorist on the scene will have at least one less logical possibility to consider as he begins work. If the model can provide, temporarily, some modicum of conceptual clarity so that the cross-cultural and cross-national inquiry into the psychopolitical aspects of man can begin, it will have served fully the purpose of its construction.

Since constructive theory building is a developing art, an overall outline of the exercise and its goals may usefully stand here as introduction. The goals set for the model of political man are:

(1) That it coordinate with and complement other theories, both the whole system and individual levels.

(2) That it relate to the ongoing development of political science as a science by explicitly clarifying analytic parallels to earlier works.

(3) That it reassert—if the imperialist motive may be forgiven—the "master science" approach to politics, by cutting across the social sciences, yet retaining a political emphasis.[20]

(4) That it explain, in depth, something about human motivations; this would require a model of some sufficient complexity.[21]

In Part II, therefore, we deal with the context into which the model fits. As a matter of paying debts (not just obeisance) to the past, Lasswell and Kaplan's early contribution to systems theory is reviewed from the aspect of individual political psychology. The overarching cybernetic theory of Deutsch is analyzed to show where amplification could enhance its utility for microanalytic concerns. And finally, the reassertion of sovereignty is attempted through the political conversion of a classic in microanalytic social theory.[22]

Following the modular and dimensional explication of the model (Part III) it is tested (Part IV) through a referral of its dimensions to the extent attitudinal and psychological research literature in an attempt to determine, first, how well it fits, descriptively, and second, what new perspectives it suggests, theoretically and empirically, in respect to the problems of rampant empiricism in these areas. Lastly (Part V), this extensive approach is supplemented through an intensive use of one module in generating a political typology that amplifies the presently overworked economic or "rational man" model.

If the exercise has been successful, it has resulted in a theoretical construct

- of sufficient generality to be applicable across cultures and nations;
- of sufficient simplicity and economy to be useful, schematically and heuristically, in empirical research;
- of sufficient complexity to cope with a wide range of human political behavior;
- and of sufficient precision so that it can be found wrong and so allow changes, deletions and amplifications to be made as the empirical returns come in.

II. THE POLITICAL FRAMEWORK

APPROACHES TO MAN . . .

The interest in political man did not disappear in the post-Platonic era not again to reemerge until the present century, but the question did thereafter get involved in the Christian worldview, a theological entanglement from which it still has trouble disengaging. Following the Renaissance redefinition of secular man,[23] the area of "political psychology" returned in the disguise of the "state of nature."[24] While the definition of "natural man" for these Enlightenment theorists was born in the course of scientific inquiry, it tended to end in polemic, obscuring the fact that the motive impetus to their search was a simple attempt to clear away the complexities (and corruptions) surrounding the human beings among whom they lived in order better to see what the basic human nature was, with which they could work in building a political system.

And the definition of the state of nature did serve to set the paradigm of the time.[25]

By the present day the combined efforts of various scientific disciplines have stripped the "natural" human material down about as far, it would seem, as it can go—either to a naked ape,[26] or to a Skinner-boxed baby, or to that modern version of Newtonian mechanism, the computer. Whichever definition he may favor, the psychopolitical theorist finds that the task of turning this *tabula rasa* into a complex, "civilized" citizen is almost entirely his responsibility—there are few if any constraints on, or inherent foundations for, the superstructure of his model. The pure psychologist may be content to map the intricacies of a single individual by means of lists of peculiar characteristics and habits,[27] but for the comparative political psychologist a theoretically more extensive approach is needed. The theory must tell the research scientist the kinds of information he needs to have about any individual to map that individual and others in such a way that he is able to deal with the questions he finds important and is led to other perhaps overlooked areas of potential importance to his work—within a theoretical matrix that provides a broad context for policy planning and research coordination.

While the scientist engrossed in difficult empirical questions, whatever his discipline, presumably finds the theory at his disposal inadequate—at least until that day when a colleague develops something equivalent to $e = mc^2$—this is rarely to say that no theory exists. It says rather that what is available does not quite suit his needs. Rejecting, as we have done, the notion that theory is built only after Epiphanic insight,[28] the solution to the inadequacies of available political theory involves then: (1) location of the most appropriate (i.e., least imperfect) theory or theories; (2) delineation of which aspects can be used and which are incomplete or not useful; and (3) modification, amplification, and combination of the parts into a new theoretical structure. This process,[29] in light of the development of the present model, we sketch in the following section.

... AND TO THEORY

The first and most broadly useful theory, within the present focus of inquiry, is one which developed in conjunction with the regnant paradigm for political science, "systems theory," and yet provides a capacity for microanalysis generally lacking to that approach. Deutsch's cybernetic theory (Deutsch, 1963) combines the general framework of the systems school with the individual flavor of the decision-making school, as well as a computer- and communications-oriented link connecting it to some of the more advanced work in information theory.[30] To make clear the remarkable richness of the model we have analytically separated it (see Figure 1, from Deutsch, 1963: 258) into its two major aspects. Figure 1 shows the "information flow" aspect, which is in line with the usual systems approach.

To highlight the major aspect of Deutsch's model for the present work, the "will" or "control" flow is shown separately in Figure 2. This aspect is critical to Deutsch's work because it provides the cybernetic or self-steering capacity that makes the system capable of autonomy—capable that is, of setting goals, striving for them, and recognizing goal achievement. As may be seen, it is largely a counter flow, working backward where the information flow works forward; this provides the basis for an empirical definition of psychological equilibrium, and eliminates the Pavlovian stigma of the simple stimulus-response model.

Of particular importance are the various "screens" that function to control:

(1) selective attention to current information

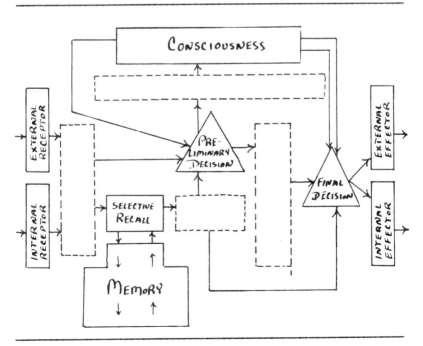

Figure 1.

    (2) acceptable recalls from memory

    (3) acceptable summary information for inspection

    (4) acceptable and feasible policies [Deutsch, 1963: 260].

These screens may be seen as controlling:

    (1) how ego perceives the world, what is relevant and acceptable, what irrelevant and unnoticed, in cognitive terms

    (2) how much information is included in ego's history and how much of it is available for current decision

    (3) how the "abstraction" and "recombination" of information proceeds, i.e., how a "raw" event is processed, what significance does it receive within the individual psychic context

    (4) what are the "moral" constraints on the goal-seeking and problem-solving activity of the decision system.

This extensive structuring gives to the model its capacity to cope with psychological reality; it also elicits a sense of there being a "ghost in the machine," for in no precise way is it clear how the screens are established, or change, or how they work, or where the source of control over them

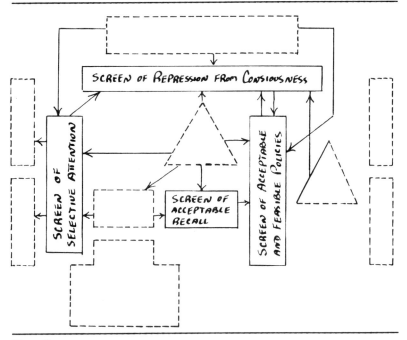

Figure 2.

lies. After some close inspection of the patterns of flow as Deutsch details them, one finally concludes that the residual "black box" is memory—through which almost everything goes, and out of which things come, and within which decisions are made affecting the entire system, but about the internal structure of which we are told very little.

In terms of the theory-modification steps outlined above, thus, it seems that in order to develop the cybernetic framework into a broad-gauge psychological model, it will be necessary to provide more structure and substance for the memory area, using as guide to this task the functions (as outlined by Deutsch) it serves for the model as a whole—particularly the control of the screens.

A similar orientation and a complementary theoretic step can be found in Lasswell and Kaplan's (1950) *Power and Society,* which may be seen in hindsight as the first pronouncement of systems theory in its political form.[31] The following excerpts are relevant to the current problem:[32]

— A person is an actor characterized as to personality (13).

> The personality is the totality of the personality traits pertaining to the actor (13).

> A personality trait is a kind of act characteristic of a self ("an act typically performed . . . in a certain kind of situation") (13).

— "The self is the ego and whatever it identifies with ego (12).

> Identification is the process by which a symbol user symbolizes his ego as a member of some aggregate or group of egos (11).

—An attitude is an "externalized" perspective (25).

> A perspective is a pattern of identifications, demands and expectations (25) "demands" are "expressions of valuation"; expectations are beliefs about actual occurrences/nonoccurrences (16, 17, 21).

These definitions serve to clarify: (1) political personality as characteristic *behavioral patterns,* (2) political identification and aggregation as functions of *symbolic patterns,* and (3) political society as a field of mutual *expectation patterns.* Thus the stage would be set for a theoretical progression from the analysis of the single actor, through intermediate social group formation, to the development of the state—had we but a framework for measuring the various patterns called for.

The most completely explicated development of this microanalytic perspective can be found in the "general theory of action,"[33] which seems, by its detailed delineation of the complexities of individual human behavior, to have precluded its own utility.[34] While a full discussion is beyond our scope here, a schematic outline is necessary. Considered analytically, the "actor" (the unit upon which the investigator chooses to focus) has three modes of motivational orientation: cognitive (he is able to perceive things), cathectic (he needs things), and evaluative (he decides whether the two previous modes can be allowed to operate directly or whether some further consideration is necessary. The evaluative mode here acts as a filter; if gratification can be allowed free rein, no further processing is necessary). If the actor determines that evaluation is called for, another system is called into play (the normative mode). Activity of this mode is assumed in the study of human actors "because we are not beasts."[35]

The evaluative mode, which may be conceived here as an "internalized" (in the psychological sense) cultural system, or an individual belief system, has three submodes corresponding to those of the motivational system, as follows:

(1) Cognitive submode: containing beliefs about persons, society, nature and the object world, and traditions; "existential beliefs," and "cognitive symbols."

(2) Appreciative submode: containing "expressive symbolization of responses to" persons, society, nature and the object world, and tradition.

(3) Normative submode: containing cognitive norms (for solving problems in (1) above), appreciative norms (for solving problems in (2) above), and moral norms dealing with overall integration problems of the actor.

Consider, by way of illustration, a hungry man. He perceives objects around him (cognitive mode of motivational orientation), and decides he needs further criteria for selecting what to eat; this latter choice brings in the evaluative mode where, say, his cognitive submode aids in designating what is edible among the array of objects; his appreciative mode influences his choice and style of eating; and his moral mode reminds him to stop before becoming overfull. And while this sort of description may seem grotesque in its detail, it does serve partially to explain why he doesn't eat the chair.

The remaining question, and the one that will conclude our Promethean exercise in theft, involves the internal dimensions of these modes; it is not sufficient to inquire *how* someone perceives his world or evaluates his actions without providing some language in which the answer can be given, some terms in which the answer can be described. Providing categories of response, or dimensions of possible difference, gives us at least a beginning to setting up the logical possibilities for internal structure, so that we can say—as a start—there are "$2n$" possible ways to perceive, or to evaluate, or whatever. This is perhaps the theorist's only defense against his own rampant eclecticism and his ability to create self-fulfilling theory.

A set of dimensions of this sort, highly formal and thus prospectively useful across the array of screens or modes, was presented in the original "action theory" outline (Parsons and Shils, 1951: 48) as defining the set of choices that the actor must make in order to fully specify his actions. These "pattern variables," whatever their "deductive" aspect, plainly derive from prior social analyses and do appear to define enduring dimensions of choice.[36] These three which will be utilized in the present model are described as follows:[37]

(1) whether direct gratification is possible, or whether some discipline is necessary;

(2) whether the actor is to orient himself to "self," in making the decision, or whether some "other" is to be considered; and

(3) what type of rule is to apply to his choice: a rule depending on particularistic criteria, or one involving abstract rules.

Parsons and Shils maintain, as does the present approach, that all the choices must be made in each decision; no choice of one of the polarities precludes choice of the other. Using the earlier example, for instance, the evaluative decision "that direct gratification is possible" does not end the decision process: the actor, having decided he can eat, still must select the way in which he does it—politely, gluttonously, omnivorously, selectively, etc. Perhaps more pertinently, the agitator who has decided to throw the rock (i.e., gratifying himself) must still decide on a target and on the degree of damage he intends. The logical possibilities resultant from combination of these three dichotomies produce eight "types" of patterned choice, as follows:[38]

Type		Dimension 1	D2	D3
Type	000	affectivity	other	particularism
	001	affectivity	other	universalism
	010	affectivity	self	particularism
	011	affectivity	self	universalism
	100	discipline	other	particularism
	101	discipline	other	universalism
	110	discipline	self	particularism
	111	discipline	self	universalism

The Parsonian terms are retained here for their generality; in the following discussion each is somewhat revised (or, more accurately, applied) from the perspective of the political problems and concerns involved. The schema, however, will provide a constant typological matrix, used repetitively in each of the modules, that allows for the combination of two theoretically useful qualities—complexity and simplicity.[39]

III. DESCRIPTION OF THE MODEL

The pattern variable scheme permeates the modes of orientation, according to action theory; therefore for each category below, paradigmatic man is assumed to make three choices (or to have a habitual predisposition toward three choices) giving him a nominally measurable score for each.

ELEMENTS OF THE MODEL

1. Cognitive beliefs concerning:
   man
   society
   nature, or object world
   tradition

2. Appreciative beliefs concerning:
   man
   society
   nature, or object world
   tradition

3. Normative system, concerning:
   cognitive norms
   expressive norms
   moral-integrative norms

The following exposition of each of these systems is to be read as cross-sectional in reference: it is designed to be used in the systematic description of man's politically relevant orientations at some *one* point in time.[40]

COGNITIVE BELIEFS

For the usual human being, "cognitive beliefs"[41] are what he calls "reality"—those definitional "self-evidents" that provide the basis for his world view.[42] The individual's particular pattern on each of the four[43] "objects of orientation" will be, variously, a function of his culture, society and roles, and his own history. Thus, while a society may be described according to "modal" patterns of cognitive beliefs, it may be hypothesized that instances of all patterns are possible within a single social group.[44] While full discussion of the implications of pattern variations in cognitive belief sets may be postponed until the exposition is complete, some preliminary notes may be useful.

An individual may hold *any* pattern of beliefs in each of the four object directions: man, society, object world, and tradition. That is, in the conveniently partitioned mind most of us have, he may believe that man is a pleasure-seeking, social individual clearly defined in terms of his social and group relations; while recognizing abstractly that society is, for example, organized on disciplined, self-oriented, universalistic lines.[45]

Differences, perhaps only gradually appreciated, on the gratification-discipline dimension hypothetically could cause severe social strain when the gratification-oriented individual comes in contact with a discipline-focussed object world. Further, the final dimension—particularism-universalism—is an obvious source of notions of social justice or injustice in those cases where, for example, cognitions of "all men are equal" meet a tradition specifying some hierarchical form of organization.

Concerning Man

Assuming that the individual defines man[46] analogously to the way his parents or events have defined him (by attitude and/or action) so that "definition of man" and "self-definition" are related, the first dimension of choice may be described as that between freedom and restraint. Either he believes *in general* he is free to do rather as he chooses; or alternatively, that he must almost always be guided by external or internal restraints. Operationally, the question may be asked: does he act for the sake of the action alone, or does he discipline himself to the activity in order to reach some other goal?[47]

The second choice dimension involves the question of whether man (or self) is defined as solitary (self-oriented) or social (other-oriented).[48] This is behaviorally a matter of whether he prefers solitude to society (society here defined as $n \geq 2$), and quasi-ethically a question of where his "proper" allegiance is seen to rest in the case of conflict.[49] In terms of the pattern model, this dimension builds upon the first dimension to clarify its implications. If the first choice was freedom, the second dimension clarifies how that freedom is perceived by the individual as something naturally to be exercised socially, with, that is, people; or as freedom "to go his own way." If alternatively the first choice was restraint, this choice clarifies the reason for the restraint: either *social* requirement or *individual* necessity.

The third distinction is between the definition of man in terms of "universalistic" or "particularistic" criteria. Universalistic definitions here might include such beliefs as the Stoic's "all men are brothers" or definitional concepts such as "virtuous." The particularistic definitions would be based on physical characteristics, or in terms of concepts at a low level of abstraction;[50] prominent would be designations in terms of nationality, religion, race, and socioeconomic class.[51]

The concatenation of this dimension with the two preceding ones completes the basic module[52] for the description of cognitive beliefs about man. Some *possible* interpretations of the eight types[53] may be illustrated with a hypothetical set of local government officials.

The first distinction would separate those who saw the position as a natural outlet for their energies (their business leaving spare time) and those who saw it as a "duty" or "necessity" for some as yet unspecified reason.

The former group, if ordered to self, would engage in satisfying personal goals; if oriented to group, would emphasize social aspects of the job. Similarly, the duty-oriented might see the post as a means to *personal* advancement, or to achievement of *group* aims.

Adding the third dimension further specifies the definition: the natural and self-oriented might satisfy particularistic aims such as better roads around *his* farm; or universalistic ones such as efficiency. The duty-oriented, collective group might put their energies into "cleaning up town hall," if elected by "public-spirited" citizens (presumably here a universalistic criterion), or may particularistically aid his (ethnic or religious) group in "getting a piece of the pie."

Concerning Society

The first distinction is one more common to political philosophers, but may be seen as implicit in the beliefs of even the man in the street. The individual viewing society will either see it as a phenomenon held together by natural human need or affection, or as an artificial construct. In the first case, it can be left to its own growth and development, largely without restraint; in the second, it requires some sort of contract or discipline to maintain it.[54]

Whatever position is taken here, the second distinction remains open: does one see society as organized for the ends of the individual member; or does the whole society, and its general needs, come first? This is a common explicit dimension in political theory; but it also arises implicitly in daily political practice: e.g., does a government order, like a draft notice, get unquestioning obedience (self in service of society), or is it protested as unacceptable to the individual's different priorities (society in service of self)?

The third distinction answers the question "what are the structural rules of society?" Is it organized on particularistic lines, as in the village "parochial" view, or the classic "aristocracy"; or is it organized on universalistic criteria, as in the "government of laws, not men?"[55]

While the third dimension is widely used and straightforward in interpretation, the effect of combining the first two may need to be clarified. A belief that society is natural, if (1) combined with a belief that the individual has primacy (when some conflict occurs), would yield a willingness to insist upon one's rights (since society is natural and not easily shaken). If (2) it is combined with a sense that society's integrity overshadows any individual's claim, one has the model of the communal society. The universalistic-particularistic dimension would complete the typology by defining the mode of organization.

If, alternatively, society is seen as artificial and contractual, the belief that the individual has primacy may be more dangerous to assert in case of conflict, as shown in the question: Will my assertion cause collapse of the whole, leaving me worse off than I am now, under some relatively minor injustice? The belief that society is artificial when combined with a belief that group rights have precedence suggests an entirely other-directed society where any dissent is deemed almost intolerable and is severely sanctioned.

Concerning the Physical World

Sensitivity to this object-orientation is found primarily among anthropologists, who are exposed to sharper differences than social scientists working within a single cultural milieu, although the latter have dealt with it tangentially, as will be noted.

As before, the first choice involved is between a perception of the object world as gratifying or not.[56] Given the wide array of possible aspects of the object world (ranging from climate to government), in an empirical study, this dimension undoubtedly would be directed to a narrower range of events. As we hope to show, however, it provides useful discrimination among belief types.

The second choice is that between self and collectivity interpreted here as an answer to the question of whether the individual perceives himself as an integral part of the object world (considers that he and, for example, nature, form a collectivity) or is independent of it. One might adduce as an illustration the reverential attitude of the American Indian toward the natural world, versus a purely exploitative attitude to the utilization of natural resources.

The third dimension is one frequently employed in cross-cultural studies, where it has had from the beginnings of anthropology in the twentieth century a strong Western bias.[57] This distinction is between perceiving the operation of the object world in universalistic terms—illustrated by Western science in its broadest terms—or perceiving it in terms of relation to self, however that self is defined. This latter attitude might be illustrated by totemism or a belief in astrology.

The derived typology, again focussing on the first two distinctions, would develop as follows: (1) the object is gratificatory and (a) man is conceived as part of it (collective attitude), leading to a sort of natural harmony and quietism; or (b) man is separate from it, leading to the exploitative or utilitarian approach already mentioned. If (2) the object is nongratifying and (a) ego feels itself part of that object, the product might be stoicism of some type; or (b) if he feels separate, the product might be alienation or a desire to conquer the object. In any of these four cases, the style of operation could involve either particularistic norms—for example, conquest-propitiation through burnt sacrifices—or universalistic norms, for example, conquering through scientific knowledge.[58]

Concerning Tradition

Tradition, while perhaps appearing a sort of object and therefore included implicitly in the foregoing module of cognitive beliefs, deserves separate treatment for several reasons: most pertinently here, that as an aspect of culture it frequently plays a decisive role in shaping political events[59] by (1) setting the parameters and constraints of action or (2) providing alternative patterns of political discourse and bargining.

On the usual three dimensions, tradition first may be perceived by the individual as gratificatory or not; and second, he may or may not see himself as part of it. The third dimension answers the question: on what terms does the tradition make its definitions? Is the individual defined in terms of universalistic criteria or particularistic ones?[60] Universalistic criteria may be such self-evident truths as "all men have inalienable rights" no matter who they are or what they do. Alternatively, particularistic criteria relate to special individuals with special needs. This may include norms favoring the rich, or a general tradition differentiating in favor of the underdog.

With respect to the political tradition, a belief that it is gratificatory to the individual and does define him as part of the society might lead to diffuse allegiance, while gratification, although ego is not a part, might produce a sort of contingent acceptance or willing coexistence;[61] each case again also varies on the third dimension.

Those for whom the tradition is nongratificatory might either (a) nonetheless see themselves as a part of it and remain in willing subjugation, or (b) see themselves outside it and either revert to a counter-tradition or seek to fulfill the requirements necessary for entrance. If entrance is impossible because one cannot, for example, meet the particularistically defined criteria, some sort of protest attitude would be hypothesized, its exact form to depend on other patterns within the individual model.

APPRECIATIVE BELIEFS

In the adaptation here of the action-theory model to the needs of political description, the appreciative system is defined as parallel to the dimensions of the cognitive belief system, but with the substitution of "ought" for "is." The individual thus may *perceive* (cognitive belief) the fact that society particularistically excludes him for religious, racial, ethnic or other reasons; while substituting in his appreciative system a society that works on universalistic norms and to which he thus may find access. Alternatively, the individual may see society as including him on the grounds of wealth and family name; and if he has no objection to this, his appreciative dimensions would coincide with his cognitive ones. A preliminary test of psychic (and potentially social) dissonance would be the degree to which cognitive and appreciative systems failed of equivalence.

This module thus provides a second broad range for mapping paradigmatic man's attitudes and internal conflicts in attitudes. The goal-seeking or decision-making process, depending on the situation, would involve a working through not only of conflicts within cognitive beliefs, but also of appreciative attitudes and of differences between the two modes.[62]

THE NORMATIVE SYSTEM

The final aspect of the model is the normative system, which might be called the "monitor." Using the same three dimensions, it sets norms of cognition influencing the content of the cognitive belief set discussed earlier; expressive norms relating to style; and general integrative rules, for coping with or mediating conflicts between alternatives.[63]

Cognitive Norms

Cognitive norms are perhaps the most critical aspect of the model because they serve as gatekeepers of all input; and, in representing the most abstract level of ideology,[64] require the greatest heroism on the part of the theorist who reduces them to binary choice level. In summary utility, the following definitions, however, did seem fruitful.

The first choice, freedom versus restraint, is in this context defined[65] as the difference between the believer and the skeptic. That these choices are relative—no one is a complete skeptic or a complete believer—is admitted, and is clarified by the definition of the other two choice dimensions.[66]

The self-collectivity division distinguishes the source of validation used by various individuals when there is some question of what to believe. The choice will be between validation by group opinion or by individualistic reliance on the self and its experiences. At the scientific level, this is the distinction between an acceptance of Pearsonian correlation coefficients at "levels established by experience" (i.e., by the professional peers) as significant and the Cartesian notion that "I'll know the truth when I see it." [67]

The third choice further ramifies the cognitive norm pattern by providing for the hoary division between those who define the real as abstract, formal, and timeless; and those who define it in terms of the unique, particular, ruggedly empirical event.[68]

The broad decision of any individual on the belief-skepticism dimension is obviously a function of childhood and youth socialization processes, and in some cases, modification continues into adulthood as new roles are acquired or defined and new events occur. Development of a predisposition towards belief is perhaps easiest to explain. The child, as De Jouvenel (1963: 48-54) suggests, has a tendency to "look up" for advice, and finding that, for instance, he indeed has been burned by a stove he had been warned not to touch, acquires a tendency to believe much of what he is told. The authority thus instituted takes on for the future a more general role in which other suitable authority sources are defined, implicitly or explicitly.

Skepticism, it may be tentatively suggested, comes about in two major ways: (1) when the authorities encourage disbelief ("you musn't believe everything you hear"); or (2) through the failure of authoritative pronouncements to accord with fact. If, that is, one does *not* get burned by the stove, the weight of further warning is decreased (the "boy who cried 'wolf' " phenomenon). At a later stage, this second approach to skepticism may be a function of intelligence—the intellectual energy that enables the individual to make comparisons between the word and the fact.[69]

The second dimension, involving the source of cognitive validation, crosscuts the first by specifying (1) for the believer, where he is to get his facts—from personal experience, or external authorities (whether one is, for example, a mystic or a churchman); and (2) for the skeptic, whether he uses his mind to seek out answers (for he must have some practical solution or, like Pyrrho, be reduced to inanity), or instead seeks until he finds some external authority to save him.[70]

Denoting the parameters of the real, the third dimension provides necessary explication in all of the above cases, as defining styles of thought that form one basis for intellectual consensus/dissensus. In the social science world of discourse, for instance, it distinguishes between those who see man as a subject for scientific inquiry and those others who see such a project as not so much immoral as *impossible.* [71]

Expressive Norms

That style is frequently more important than substance in various forms of political activity is well known. Candidates insist on discussing "the issues," while voters with equal persistence vote "for the man." Some of the broader dimensions of this latter process can be encompassed in the following outline. (Others are a function of the total model.)

First, is the preference for individual behavior that is natural, open, emotional; or for behavior that is disciplined and/or restrained? Second, is the behavioral style oriented in terms of group norms, or in individualistic-eccentric terms? Third, is the style abstract, pure, simple, and perhaps elegant; or is it profuse, rich, colorful, and complex?

The second distinction separates, at the institutional level, the "party man," who places group cohesion and loyalty in a central position, from the maverick.

The other two dimensions, as they crosscut each other, might be illustrated by two natural, expressive types—Eisenhower and Johnson— who diverge on the third dimension as, respectively, stylistically simple versus stylistically complex. Two restrained figures might be Nixon (simplicity) and Eugene McCarthy (complexity).

Moral Norms

In order to maintain the individualistic level of analysis, definitions within this module expressly reject the Parsonian interpretation of its serving a mediating role between the needs of the individual and of the social whole. We have instead defined the choices solely in terms of the individual's problems in integrating his own desires, and allowed the question of social integrative needs to be solved by his position in the earlier-defined cognitive belief categories. That some of the end-goals defined here may involve the individual with some larger unit does not attenuate the individualistic perspective.

The first dimension hypothesized in the establishment of these broad value parameters is the same as in preceding instances; here interpreted in terms of a choice between the search for complete gratification of some type, or the acceptance of some limitations or discipline bounding the goal.[72] The distinction might be illustrated as that between Nietzsche's (1961) model of unending transcendence and Thomas More's (1964) Utopian disciplining of "pleasure" into the balance-harmony of "happiness."

The second distinction becomes here a question of whether the goal state involves the individual alone or some other. The individual, for instance, might choose to seek wealth solely for the personal prestige he expects it to produce; or, might select "personal salvation," or the other-oriented goal of developing a stable religious community.[73] Alternatively, the choice may be illustrated as the difference between "sauve-qui-peut" and "greater love hath no man than to give up his life for a friend."

Finally, the individual is presumed to have a choice along the particularism-universalism dimension. Are his goals to be couched in terms of immediacies directly related to his own physical needs and desires, or in terms of broad, more abstract categories?[74]

In the following (Part IV), we turn to a consideration of research relevant to the areas encompassed by the model; readers interested primarily in a preliminary theoretic summarization and the model's implications will find the discussion in Part V more useful.

IV. ANALYSIS OF RESEARCH

In this section, we consider the model in relation to the literature of the political and other social sciences; our purpose is to suggest that the schema we have outlined is (1) sufficient to encompass most of the concepts now in common use, and (2) capable of providing a classificatory organization to a presently disorganized world of discourse in this area of political man and his attributes. Our underlying premise is, of course, that until some order has been brought to the problem, there is no hope of (a) knowing clearly what it is that we in fact know about man, or (b) deciding what points need clarification and further investigation. It is this benchmark function the model is intended primarily to serve.

A systematic approach to the miscellany of work relevant to political man generally might take either a formal route—based on the conceptual level used—or a substantive one—utilizing the subject area as a source of coherence. The former is precluded in the present case because of the ambiguity of concept formation common to most of the work: whether one is dealing with a *trait, attitude, dimension, characteristic, type,* or *value* is rarely clear; nor does any arbitrary solution seem feasible or useful. The substantive approach falls into the difficulty the model is designed to avoid as far as possible—the bias introduced by the normative concerns of the investigator,[75] which while natural and desirable has in the area of political man tended to produce a naive Manicheanism destructive to the process of inquiry.

The discussion below therefore slights conceptual level, dealing with most terms according to adjectival significance only. The concepts included are taken from the following list, given alphabetically for reference purposes, then grouped as seemed convenient in terms of natural clustering and the requirements of exposition.[76]

Achievement 1(i)
acquiescence 2(i)
aggression 2(i)
alienation 3(i)
allegiance 3(i)
ambiguity tolerance-intolerance 1(ii)
anxiety 1(i)
authoritarianism 3(i)
awareness 3(i)

Bohemianism 1(ii)n.

Calvinism 3(i)n.
chauvinism 2(iv)
competence 1(i)n.
contempt for weakness 2(i)n.
cynicism 2(iii)n.

Democratic attitudes 3(i)
deviance 3(i)
direct action 3(ii)
dogmatism 1(ii)
dominance 2(ii)

Efficacy 3(i)n.
egalitarian-elitism 2(i)n. and 3(ii)
ego strength 1(i)
ethnocentrism 2(iv)
extremism 3(ii)

Faith in people 2(iii)
futility 3(i)n.

Guilt 1(i)

Hostility 2(i)

Impotence 3(i)n.
independence of government 3(ii)n.
inflexibility 1(ii)
initiative 1(i)n.
intellectuality 1(ii)n.
intolerance of human frailty 2(i)n.

isolation 3(i)
issue familiarity 1(i)n.

Left-right attitudes 3(ii)
liberalism-conservatism 3(ii)
life satisfaction 1(i)n.
localism-cosmopolitanism 3(ii)n.

Machiavellianism 2(iii)n.
meaninglessness 3(i)
misanthropy 2(iii)n.
mysticism 1(ii)n.

Need inviolacy 1(i)
normlessness 3(i)
nostalgia 3(ii)n.

Open-closed mind 1(ii)
optimism-pessimism 1(i)n.

Paranoia 2(i)
parochialism 3(i)n.
participation 3(i)n.
philistine 1(ii)
powerlessness 3(i)
protestant ethic 3(i)n.

Radicalism 3(ii)n.
responsibility 3(i)n.

Self-confidence 1(i)n.
self-esteem 1(i)n.
self-estrangement 3(i)
status frustration 1(i)n.
strongmindedness 1(ii)

Tolerance 3(i)
totalitarian 3(i)
tough-tender minded 1(ii)n.
traditional 3(ii)n.
trust in people 2(iii)

Underdog identification 3(ii)n.

ATTRIBUTES OF INDIVIDUAL

The list of qualities, attributes, and orientations pertaining to the single individual, more or less *in vacuo,* falls into two major clusters: (1) one centered on individual integration with, or adaptation to, the environment (e.g., ego strength, self-confidence, self-esteem, competence, achievement) and the alternative failure patterns (anxiety, bewilderment, cynicism, guilt, need-inviolacy); (2) the other on rigidity (dogmatism, closed-mindedness, inflexibility, intolerance of ambiguity, philistinism) and its less clear obverse (open-mindedness, strong-mindedness, bohemianism, tolerance of ambiguity). While close inspection may suggest the clusters converge at the operational level, they may serve as useful foci for discussion.

Ego Strength

This concept, while central to psychoanalysis, psychology, and social psychology since their inception and thus far too complex for depth coverage here, also appears explicitly in some political studies and is implicit in many more.[77] Since it is generally classified as an 'emotional' factor, and tends to recall always the plight of the Freudian ego trapped between warring id and superego, it is perhaps surprising to see that the present model—which does not purport to cover 'emotions'—in the event does subsume much of the content of ego strength within its categories.

As used by McCloskey and Schaar (1965: 30), the factor is defined in terms of dominance, self-confidence, and life satisfaction, and—negative-ly—in reference to alienation, futility, guilt, need inviolacy, pessimism, and status frustration; we will concentrate here on those subconcepts primarily related to the individual, dealing with the dyadic and systemic aspects under their proper headings.

The primary positive subconcepts of self-confidence, self-esteem, and personal competence involve much overlap at the conceptual level, and some confusion at the operational one. Yet since the tests are subjective and self-anchoring, they tap the individual's general sense of "security in his world" (whatever that world may be).[78] What does not emerge clearly from any of the studies is the objective, contextual relationship of the subjective attitude. There is a difference between the individual who thinks himself incompetent but in fact copes rather effectively with a diverse environment and the one who thinks himself incompetent and actually is. If the psychologist can find reason to lump these and other mixed types together in the same category, surely the political scientist cannot; it would make a mockery of either explanation or prediction.

Because illness is clearer than health, and far easier to define, no overall solution to the "ego strength" problem will be provided here; rather, some basic approaches to solution based on the dimensions of the model. First, the model provides terms for describing the individual and his society and for postulating the degree of ego threat or the scope of the troubles the individual is likely to encounter. Second, it can define the extent to which the individual faces the same problems as other individuals (Campbell, 1958: 41-45) who share his beliefs and "definition of the situation" and the resultant probability of social and psychological support. Third and most useful, from the definitional perspective, the model allows a systematic approach to the terms of the individual's strength, esteem, and confidence (or lack thereof).[79] It could be said then, that because an individual's cognitive perceptions concerning himself converge with his chosen preferential pattern (all described in the model's dimensional terms), the probability of his standing well in his own estimate is high; if that preferential pattern is also one held by a majority of his group (again described in terms of the model), then the probability of social esteem reinforcing self-esteem increases the likelihood of an even higher self-standing. Various other situations could be dealt with similarly.[80]

Another concept included in this general "ego strength" cluster—the motivation to achieve—would be a special case of this situation, containing both individual and social components.[81] The model would allow, in addition, a clarification of the type of achievement, primarily in terms of the moral mode (distinguishing, for example, between achievement in economic vs. religious spheres) and other elements of the normative system.

The obverse side of this particular cluster, in addition to the subconstructs discussed elsewhere, may be illustrated by the concepts of guilt, need inviolacy, and anxiety.

We do not attempt here to trace the history of "guilt" as a psychological or psychoanalytic term but accept the simple definition "sense of having committed a wrong." The emotion or guilt then becomes a function of an individual's commission of some act inconsonant with his belief system. The question of *why* his behavior did not fit his beliefs (if beliefs are of scientific interest, it can only be because they relate to overt behavior) may be seen either (1) as a conflict between his cognitive and preferential beliefs or (2) as a failure in the individual's interpretation of the situation that led to misapplication of the believed criteria.

Need inviolacy involves "the individual's desire to maintain his status and protect himself from the intrusions of others."[82] While this is not covered in the model as presented (i.e., in terms of describing a cross-section of a system prefatory to dynamic analysis or modelling) it could be incorporated as a "tolerance level" for acquiescence, for example. Hypothetically, it may be predicted that certain belief and norm patterns have a higher level of tolerance than others (e.g., a gratification-oriented "maximizer" may have lower levels of tolerance than a discipline-oriented "moderator").[83]

The concept "anxiety," though more common to clinical literature than to the political,[84] raises some interesting questions as one attempts to deal with it in terms of the present model. Defined through the component concepts of "excessive worry," "restlessness," and "inability to concentrate" (McCloskey, 1967: 71), anxiety fits none of the dimensions. As a speculative explanation, we would postulate anxiety as a behavioral response to a pattern system in "imbalance":[85] a system, that is, in which most or all of the choices on the first dimension emphasize discipline or, on the second dimension, a self-orientation. There are obviously unstated premises involved in such hypotheses, but while answers will only come from actual research, it seems not unreasonable to assume that in fact men require *some* gratification, or some group orientations; as "we are not beasts," so we are not machines.

Identification and investigation of these functional correlates of model types undoubtedly will clarify the range of patterns functional and dysfunctional for the individual, leading eventually to normative judgments not presently included.[86]

Dogmatism-rigidity Cluster

The second of the major clusters of concepts relating to the individual in his approximate solitude is the one centering on various types of rigidity; the types in this case being so various as to reach ambiguously to the opposite pole, as "strongmindedness."[87] Again, the connotations of the terminological area derive from Freud, with the "inflexibility index" of McCloskey (1967: 69-70) based on the standard anal characteristics of reaction-formation, rationalization, projection, and denial. Similarly pejorative was the description of "philistine" man (Thomas and Znaniecki, 1965: 934-935) by a fixed attitude structure, conservatism, and severe intellectual limitations. The alternative to dogmatic man was again more elusive; clearly an open mind was more desirable than pigheadedness, but to most investigators, pure flexibility of attitude was less important, at least implicitly, than the substantive acceptability of the attitude cluster.[88] "Democratic man," if he turned out to be stubborn about something, was more apt to be termed strongminded than dogmatic, though exceptions did occur.

The most clear treatment conceptually of this concept cluster as it relates to broadly political questions has been provided by the psychologist Milton Rokeach (1960: 55-56). Rokeach's definition has three aspects: a formal one, involving the individual's knowledge about other belief systems and his magnitude of rejection of beliefs he does not hold; a substantive one, involving attitudes toward the world and toward authority; and a third, distinguishing perspectives on time.

With respect to the formal aspect of this definition[89] three subcomponents are distinguished: intensity[90] of rejection; difference in differentiation between belief and disbelief systems; and the individual's overall intercommunication between the two systems. While Rokeach has usefully investigated some of the experimental aspects of the questions raised, many of the theoretical or conceptual problems continue troublesome in the explanation (as distinguished from the description) of such attitudes as prejudice. Nor does the questionnaire technique elicit from respondents anything analytically useful. Catholics and Episcopalians mutually perceive each other as "similar" in belief, and Baptists most dissimilar to themselves (among Christian groups). The criteria on which the decision is made, however, remain vague (Rokeach, 1960: Ch. 16).

What is needed, we would argue, is a framework such as that provided by the present model which allows the *investigator* greater analytic leverage in the study of such perceived differences. If an investigator seeking to estimate possible social conflict is restricted to asking members of the two groups about their attitudes toward each other, he may elicit entirely spurious data, based on his informants' misapprehension of the situation. If on the other hand he has a vehicle—such as the present model—which permits him to take an independent approach to the question, he may be able to make a far better estimate of the probable results of bringing the two groups together in a new housing project, for example (Rokeach, 1968: Ch. 3).

The model additionally might provide a vehicle for spatially ordering the miscellany of concepts relating to open and closedmindedness by designating their functional and strategic importance in the decision-making network.[91] Ambiguity tolerance-intolerance, a construct related to the general question of rigidity, serves as an illustration. Initially related to work on the authoritarian syndrome,[92] the interpretations now range from Lane's "willingness to put up with legislative delay" to individual simplemindedness, social discomfort, patriotism, perfect value cohesion as an ideal, and even optimism.[93] This sort of conceptual overlapping[94] that apparently attempts to infuse the whole range of interesting characteristics into each partial construct is plainly self-defeating. Using the model's terms, the problem area can be clearly delineated into its component parts; specifying to the "cognitive norm" module the idea of "perception of dimensionalized stimuli as dichotomized" and the qualities of "rigid and categorical thinking;" to the "moral norm" module the qualities of "seeking unambiguous and clear solutions," and to the model's substantive sections, the questions of the nature of one's fellows and the ideal state of society.[95]

INTERPERSONAL ATTRIBUTES

In the realm of interpersonal characteristics involved in descriptions of political man, the major concepts fall under a single heading, that of aggression-dominance and its alternative—sociability-acquiesence.[96] To avoid giving a spurious coherence to the related literature, we will discuss the various aspects under the following concepts:

(1) aggression, including paranoia, hostility, intolerance of human frailty, and contempt for weakness
(2) dominance, including acquiescence
(3) faith-trust in people, including misanthropy
(4) ethnocentrism and chauvinism

Aggression

The concept of aggression raises one of the perennial contentions of political discourse—whether man is naturally aggressive, or is sociable and peaceful; whether life is "solitary, poor, nasty, brutish and short," or whether utopia is possible.[97] As operationally defined, it includes such characteristics as hostility, paranoia, intolerance of human frailty, and contempt for weakness (McCloskey and Schaar, 1965: 30-31; McCloskey, 1967).

While McCloskey designates it an emotional factor, and while the clinical term "paranoia" points to a degree of pathology the model does not hope to reach, a degree of clarification can be achieved by consideration of various types of aggressive behavior in terms of the pattern model. A tentative causal sequence may be postulated: beginning with paranoia and followed by hostility and its two subsidiary attitudes—intolerance and contempt.[98]

Paranoia, as R. D. Laing has pointed out so convincingly (Laing and Esterson, 1970), is often a misnomer for real persecution. The "paranoid" office worker turns out to be the object of actual malice on the part of colleagues; or generally, a sense of persecution may be generated when any individual (or group) finds himself "defined out" of a social situation he wishes to enter.[99] Another sort of situation conducive to a sense of persecution would be the attempt by an authority (be that parent or the political system) to impose a value system inimical to an individual. This alternative is the reverse of the former; here the situation defines the individual "in" but he prefers to be defined "out."

Two points may be noted concerning this analysis. First, there is no infinite regress to the explanation. It does not suppose that an aggressive pattern is "started by" some primal aggressor; rather it provides for "accidental" causation through *dis*congruent value systems.[100] Second, the model does not at this point attempt to explain why a particular individual finds some value systems inimical. This is a question that can only be seriously investigated when the system itself can be described with some degree of precision.

Following McCloskey, we have suggested hostility as the second stage in the aggression sequence; here it may be pointed out that this is but one of the possibilities. An "acquiescent" individual[101] may react to persecution by "converting," adopting the mores of the other. Assuming no hostility inherent in the adopted value system,[102] the persecution-aggression syndrome would then abort. For the nonacquiescent individual, the sequence may cease if the object situation provides alternative individuals or groups that do not generate hostility. Actual hostility may occur, according to this analysis, only in cases of strongminded[103] individuals who refuse to acquiesce and who find no alternative non-hostility-producing group.

Hostility having been generated, what turns it into aggression, and what forms of aggression occur? For the answer, one virtually must return to the full system described in Part III. Depending on the individual's cognitive and appreciative beliefs and normative system, he may exemplify patterns of aggression in the whole panoply of socially eu- and dys-functional behavior syndromes. The individual may turn from society and make use of his aggression in opening the frontier; he may turn it against himself and become an ascetic; he may seek to conquer the world through science or magic; and so on.[104]

Dominance

Dominance, a commonly used psychological and social term,[105] and one that lurks behind most discussions of political power, is one for which there is no special dimension provided in the model, and this is deliberate.

It would seem clearly a case of prejudgment to assume that certain individuals have an innate desire in this direction; even Hobbes' classic statement of the pattern "the restless striving of power after power which ceases only in death" (Hobbes, 1958: 86) has an empirical and thus contingent explanation—in a situation of incomplete gratification and severe uncertainty, power is a means of holding what one has and of attempting to acquire one's goals. At the level of moral norms, of course, a maximizer will tend to fit Hobbes' prediction; but under more secure circumstances than the seventeenth century a moderator may not.

In precise reference to the relationship of the concept to the model proposed, dominance raises one of the speculatively more interesting questions with which we have dealt. Is it the case, one might ask, that certain positions on any of the dimensions dominate other positions; or that certain three-dimensional patterns in any mode dominate others; or that some types, a function of all eleven areas of orientation, dominate others.[106] While answers here will be possible only when the model is converted into satisfactory operational form, a partial discussion of the possibilities may be ventured upon.

Taking the mode involving "cognitive beliefs concerning man," some of the following might serve as plausible hypotheses: (1) discipline dominates over immediate gratification, at least in certain contexts. The economic realm and problems of modernization come to mind. The disciplined individual, the one who is prepared to show up at work regularly and take direction, is able to acquire the means and goods to achieve social prominence, and if the group question is "whose advice shall we take on . . . ," the choice is more likely of him than of the pleasure-oriented man who works only as necessary and spends most of the day sitting in the sun.[107] In more complex political situations, the politician who is severely disciplined toward the goal of winning the election and follows all the rules about building at the grass roots, getting out the vote, and so on, may in a rather large number of cases dominate the less-disciplined candidate who makes excellent speeches but somehow never gets sufficiently organized to have a full audience.

(2) A self orientation dominates over other orientation. This is not to assume that one man can dominate a group, but that between any two individuals in a field of action, the self-oriented will dominate. In the simplest case, alluded to above,[108] he will dominate simply because his partner, being social, needs him to fulfill that need. If his demands are too severe, of if alternative partners are available, isolation may be the outcome rather than dominance.

Two final suggestions may be raised: at the level of cognitive norms, skepticism dominates belief unless the belief system involved is realistically oriented;[109] and at the level of moral norms, maximizers dominate moderators unless the latter are supported by a strongly maintained tradition. This is suggested by the traditional analyses of the difficulty of maintaining democracies.[110]

Faith-trust in People

Trust in people,[111] as used by the Survey Research Center, involves beliefs concerning whether men are (1) trustworthy, (2) helpful, and (3) fair. While respondents might be expected to have some difficulty in selecting a simple Yes or No on such questions,[112] clearly the question is of interest to political scientists.

In the broadest context, the question of whether one man trusts his fellows[113] would seem to be a function of the degree to which he finds himself among men who share all or most of his belief system as defined by the model. However he defines man and society, he will tend to trust those who appear to him to have similar definitions. Obviously, how far he trusts them depends on how far he trusts or would trust himself. The narrower questions of helpfulness and fairness correspond to the latter two dimensions of cognitive definition of man, the self-other and the particularism-universalism distinctions; helpfulness being assumed to imply that one perceives another to have an other-orientation (that includes him within its range), and fairness, that one anticipates universalistic criteria to be applied.[114]

What perhaps has been underestimated in the utilization of the concept is the degree to which it is a simple cognitive matter. In small, country towns one never locks the door because of certain cognitive beliefs (derived from experience) that man is disciplined (he will not impulsively gratify himself with your belongings), that he is collectively oriented (he takes your rights into account as well as his own), and that he has universalistic definitions of property rights that say a man's house is inviolate. In the city a different situation *in fact* exists, and one's lack of faith in people is similarly cognitive.

A second aspect may be noted here: while it is frequently assumed that faith in people is essential or useful to democracy, under certain circumstances it may be an ultimately dysfunctional reaction formation, as psychoanalysts use the term. That is, an individual living in a high-crime area may assert his preference (appreciative mode) to trust people by refusing to lock his door or take similar practical precautions. This sort of idealism may be a particularly American characteristic that deserves investigation in various contexts.

Ethnocentrism

The term "ethnocentrism," despite its connection with larger political syndromes,[115] basically is "conceived as an ideological system pertaining to groups and group relations," distinguishing ingroups (to which the individual belongs) from antithetical outgroups.[116] In terms of the model, it may be described as belief that groups are important in man's definition (other-orientation). This group definition in particularistic terms may be referent to caste, race, etc., or in universalistic ones, though the former is more often implied.[117]

The referential aspects of the concept (derogation of minorities) would be explicated by incremental additions to the "cognitive beliefs concerning man" module of the individual under study. The fact that the subject had a variety of definitions for man based on ethnic indicators would be *prima facie* evidence of ethnocentrism. For example, full determination of a tendency toward racism would be provided by comparing the individual's definition of outgroup man to his own ingroup definition.[118]

Chauvinism[119] would illustrate the same pattern, but the defined group would be coextensive with the national boundaries, very likely the result of having no other favorable internal group with which to identify.[120]

SOCIOPOLITICAL SYSTEMS ORIENTATIONS

Two major constellations can be discerned within the literature dealing with political man in his relationships to the total system within which he operates: (1) the contextually biased concepts relating to democratic attributes and the obverse, usually authoritarian, attributes; and (2) the related but no clearer polarity born in 1789, the left-right continuum.

Democratic Attitudes

While it would be implausible here to attempt to provide a definitional solution of the term democracy;[121] and while democratic commitment, in terms of the model, is in the American context formally equivalent to adherence to any set of traditional norms; the conceptual area does provide occasion for a discussion of a tradition in terms of the model's dimensions. It must first of all be accepted that any tradition need not be internally coherent or consistent; as Boorstin has suggested, ambiguity and even lacunae are probably useful in the long-range viability of a complex system. An aspect of this problem is the further likelihood of a distinction between the explicit tradition ("all men are created equal") and the de facto tradition (a system of slavery). This situation itself reinforces the argument that some schema is necessary for explicating the various subtraditions in a way that makes comparison and contrast possible, to enable one to say "there are n major traditions discerned, of which tradition$_1$ is professed by groups$_{1,2,20}$, ..., tradition$_2$ by groups$_{5,9,14}$, ..., tradition$_3$ by groups ..., etc." No one would predict instant or complete solution of such an extended analysis, but the primary ability to make statements of this sort seems to bear the seeds of discovery progressively open to refinement.

By way of illustration of the modes of distinguishing two democratic traditions we may, with no attempt at premature precision, offer a comparison of Thomas More's Utopia (1964) and a grossly oversimplified sketch of some U.S. norms.

(1) Cognitive beliefs concerning Man: More's Utopia is hedonistic (gratification pole), while the U.S. has been more dominated by the Calvinist ethic of discipline and constraint.[122] Utopia, on the second dimension, was socially oriented; the U.S., again in Calvinist overview, is self-oriented. Both appear to define man universalistically.[123]

(2) Cognitive beliefs concerning Society: Neither of the traditions we are discussing appear to believe that society is natural. The Utopians' founding father deliberately cut away the island and consciously established certain social patterns. One might illustrate the U.S. attitude by a maxim inculcated into the students at a New England high school (whether it is typical is of course a question): "No one has the right to do that, which if everybody did it, would destroy society." Or, more colloquially, "don't rock the boat." Implicit is the idea of fragility.[124]

On the second dimension, in case of conflict "who comes first?" the Utopians seem to select society; while opposed to war, they fight when necessary and perhaps would adhere to the old notion of "dulce et decorum." Here the U.S. position, once similar to the Utopians, is clearly, in certain sectors, shifting.

The third dimension provides another distinction between our two examplars: Utopians, so More relates, make no social distinctions—education is fine, but it is more useful perhaps to make good chairs, and even "fools are loved." Conversely, the citizens of an "achievement society" make distinctions of status and wealth.[125]

A more complete description of either tradition would continue through the other subsystems outlined earlier. We have attempted only to show, in a methodologically rather inexact sketch, that the dimensions do elicit much of the material commonly raised in such analyses, and in a form that makes protocomparison possible.

* * * * * *

The general attitude toward deviance,[126] of which the degree of tolerance for political nonconformists is a part, is rather more complex, analytically, than the usual and useful operationalization into "Do you think professed Communists should be allowed to run for office?" and similar questions.

There is, first, the question of traditional-social definition of "acceptable" roles—personal, social, and political. If this society-wide allocation is broad, there will be an appearance of tolerance and certainly a wide variety of choices of individual role, but the concept "tolerance for deviance" will be descriptive of the society, not the individual within it (who may accept the socially defined 99 roles but balk at the 100th which has been left out). Alternatively, a society may offer a narrow range of expected roles, but allow or encourage unusual (i.e., deviant) behavior; or both patterns may be reversed. These might be called "open" or "closed" societies, as distinct from the second aspect of deviance, individual open or closedmindedness.

In the context of the model offered here, this concept most directly relates to the second dimension of expressive norms, or style. Description, for any group, would be provided by answering the question, are group-"blending" types of behavior favored, or is the individual encouraged to be "eccentric," that is, self-oriented and self-defining. Only analysis through the full range of dimensions would define adequately the areas where such behavior would be allowed, in the range of roles available to the individual.

"Awareness" is one of those quasi-value-free terms, which always, at least in the American context, implies that the civics class norms are both individually and systemically desirable. As descriptive theory, this notion has declined; the reasons for its persistence as normative theory are obscure but hopefully avoided by the model, which (in social man) allows for the nonaware, nonactive, private individual.[127]

"Competence," qualified variously as civic, political or personal competence, is similar or equivalent to efficacy and participation; and obversely related to political futility, political impotence, parochialism, and cynicism—personal and political.[128]

While the conceptual area is clear enough in its operational definitions, more definition is certainly possible concerning the background configurations that may lead a respondent to state a sense of competence or efficacy. Among those possibilities, three may be explored: (1) the individual who has, by accident of circumstances (his father was mayor) or by interest, learned about the political process and enjoys participating in it as a form of social activity; (2) the individual who at some time has been threatened by an aspect of the political process and has had successful recourse to a branch of government in removing the threat; (3) the individual who has absorbed wholesale his high school civics course and firmly believes his vote and voice count, in the teeth of any and all experience to the contrary. Explication in terms of the model might be as follows.

One type of competent man (the term is used here as equivalent to an individual with a sense of efficacy) can be described most simply in terms of his cognitive beliefs about man: he believes him to be (1) free to gratify himself without larger future ends, and (2) other-oriented, i.e., a social being. Assuming the situation provides associates[129] and that he finds them responsive to himself and to his ideas, he would be expected to develop competence—personal or political, depending on his choice of level.[130]

Were such an individual to fail to find a comfortable milieu, one might hypothesize as a result neither cynicism nor futility but a shift to some plausible alternative society, perhaps family activity.[131]

Alternatively, in a situation where hitherto pleasant group activities become a course of conflict or complexity, this type of individual might lose the sense of efficacy that was primarily a spinoff from his primary goal. This qualification of competence in terms of genesis and thus prognosis has clear implications for political systems.

The second type of competent individual is a polar opposite to the foregoing on several dimensions. Presuming a definition of man as disciplined, self-oriented, and universalistically defined, his entrance to the political process would be as a means to some self-defined end, and a means to which he is entitled as a "citizen" regardless of race, religion or other particularistic factors. Further definition of his aims would be in terms of his position on the "moral norm" dimension—whether he is attempting to maximize some goals or simply to save the status quo; whether those goals are self- or group-defined; and whether they are physical or abstract. It might be predicted, for research purposes, that certain types of regimes are more successful in satisfying certain types of demands, a correlation that would aid in clarifying the relation of efficacy to the objective political process.

The third illustration of the possible forms of competence-efficacy might be a case of arrested development similar to that discussed under chauvinism,[132] or of reaction formation. In the first instance, an individual who is, in terms of cognitive norms, a "believer" with "other" validated norms, acquires certain aspects of the political tradition without questioning or testing. Depending on the shape of that tradition, he may make efficacious responses without their having any root in experience. The other case, that of reaction formation, similarly would have a purely subjective sense of efficacy in having unconsciously substituted appreciative (preferential) beliefs for cognitive ones—for example, "the system *ought* to be responsive, therefore I'm sure it *is.*"[133]

The definition of alienation, which ranges from the broadest to the narrowest,[134] is generally thought of as including powerlessness, meaninglessness, normlessness or anomie, isolation, and self-estrangement, [135] although which or how many any particular author intends is not always clear.

At a minimum, the pattern model provides basic clarification of the five subterms listed above: powerlessness relating to one's beliefs concerning a generalized world;[136] normlessness to beliefs about tradition; isolation to beliefs about society; self-estrangement to beliefs about man. Meaninglessness would involve primarily the cognitive norm system; hypothetically it would be produced either (1) when a believer was deprived of his object of belief or (2) when a skeptical mind has systematically disproved everything it has touched, and is beset with a literal meaninglessness.[137]

Furthermore, within each aspect of alienation, the model forces a breadth of description that makes it difficult to overgeneralize; dealing with the individual "estranged from self," for instance, one is led to the observation that the exact content of one's self-beliefs is irrelevant; what *is* critical is the formal congruence of cognitive and appreciative belief patterns. This also would be true for the other areas of the model; alienation is clearly contextual, and a type of man alienated in one society may be an ideal citizen in another.

It is, however, probably the case that certain polarities hold a higher probability of alienation. In terms of individual cognitive beliefs concerning self-definition, one might postulate that the disciplined is more liable to estrangement than the pleasure-oriented individual who, not looking beyond the moment, is less likely to have disappointments. Similarly, the group-oriented is more susceptible than the truly self-oriented[138] because he needs help from the contextual situation in order to fulfill his group orientation; while the self-oriented has a greater degree of independence. These are of course speculations, suitable only as possible guides to actual research.

An analogous concept—allegiance—may be viewed in a similar way to alienation: as made up of several parts corresponding to the levels of the model. Allegiance may be defined in terms of (1) self, (2) society, (3) tradition, and (4) the object world. In the first case, "self-allegiance" is an uncommon term for a common notion involving ego strength and whatever falls on the normal pole of the typology under construction. [139] The other three orientations, in a political sense, might be used as a basic scale of "degree of allegiance."[140]

The euphemistically named "authoritarian" syndrome,[141] the common antitype to democratic patterns, to a large extent has already treated here in the discussion of its component parts.[142] Therefore, we will attempt to draw the concepts together within the model by means of a developmental sketch of the authoritarian (or protofascist) man. While partial, it may suggest the architectonic qualities of the model.

Hypothetically, the syndrome may begin with the individual's being forced (disciplined) to adopt (believe in) *other*-oriented norms, that direct him to define reality as concrete (anti-intraception); and stylistically, demand discipline, group adherence, and a "tough" simplicity. With respect to the moral norm module, the individual "ideally" is told to listen to authority, rather than to adopt a fast position.[143]

Implicitly, cognitive definitions of man, of society, and of the generalized world might be postulated as follows: man—unrestrained (dangerous), selfish, particularistically (e.g., racially) defined; society— natural (perhaps corrupted), and group-defined (deviance is intolerable); the world—gratifying, collective, mystic. At several points here, actual authoritarian and/or fascist patterns would diverge and should be studied as divergent phenomena.[144]

Left Right Attitudes

Since the left-right continuum,[145] in one or another variation of nomenclature is frequently considered the equivalent of "ideology," the postponement of its consideration until the last may seem somewhat cavalier. From the foregoing definition and discussion, however, the reasons for this position should be clear: if the narrower concepts are in fact seen to be so complex, the larger concepts based on them become almost unmanageable.

The summary statement concerning the model's relation to this set of concepts would be: it provides a basis for retaining them by clarifying the full meaning of the terms. We will not attempt to do this here by means of any full investigation of the literature on the subject, which clearly would be impossible within the present constraints. Starting at the outer edges of the dimension, however, we will attempt a schematic illustration.

The concept of "extremism," while definable only in the context of an individual culture or tradition,[146] at a first approximation here may be recognized through an individual's taking a maximizing pole in defining his goals.[147] Two illustrations of political behavior generally characterized as extreme can be provided through comparison of model patterns for the stereotypical right- and left-wing individuals, although it is not our hope to find a consensually acceptable definition for these vague terms.[148]

The right-wing definition of man generally would seem to begin with discipline toward some goal; the left-wing definition, with gratification of the common man's needs. While the self-other distinction varies with the political context, it may be suggested that insofar as the right-wing pattern in this country correlates with the Protestant ethic,[149] it has a self-orientation; whereas the left is communally or other-oriented. The third dimension, again, would seem to find these two wings opposed: the right making its definitions in ethnocentric terms; the left tending toward universalistic definitions based on "universal brotherhood."[150]

Remaining in an American context, and at an impressionistic level, it is clear that these patterns are similar to what one might sketch for the "conservative" and for the "liberal." Whether such orientations become "extreme" or not would be a situational question depending on the individual's definition of the object world[151] and tradition. Critical in these two areas is undoubtedly the question of whether the individual perceives himself defined "in" or "out" by the society; the individual with a strong sense of identity it might be predicted would have greater tendency toward moderation at the moral norm level.[152]

The related concepts of egalitarianism-elitism[153] are at a first approximation defined simply as the two poles of the third dimension in defining man: egalitarianism being the universalistic definition, elitism the particularistic one. The definition, for any one individual, may vary between his cognitive and preferential modes. Additionally, there are contextual aspects without consideration of which no clear-cut interpretation of a respondent's position can be given.[154]

* * * * * *

The purpose of the survey[155] has been multiple: First, though perhaps implicitly, to suggest the terminological and conceptual weaknesses involved in research on political man; overlapping constructs, dual terminology for single phenomena, the same name given to diverse phenomena—all these make progress unlikely if not impossible.

Second, to observe the degree to which bias has beleaguered empirical research—one student's "yeoman" is another student's "protofascist"; the confrontation between the two usually results in argument rather than analysis and/or synthesis.

Finally, to suggest that the more abstractly defined dimensions of the model presented here are temporarily sufficient to assist in the task of clarifying and of filling out the conceptual area; this not by going ahead of current research, but by remaining with it to secure the lines of communication before attempting to advance.

V. TYPES OF MAN

A TYPOLOGY

Because Part IV was intended to suggest that the dimensions of the pattern model are appropriate to and sufficient for the usual world of discourse concerning political man, the discussion necessarily branched out in numerous directions over terminologically diverse empirical studies. To indicate that the model is not infinitely Protean, we now turn to a consideration of its summarizing capacities: the structural parameters it provides for the development of models of political men.[156] The goal in the development of the succeeding typology, from a utilitarian viewpoint, was a model that (1) was simple, preferably using only one module, (2) provided a place for the economic or "rational" type, which has been widely adopted in the profession, and (3) amplified somewhat the range of types available, by generating alternatives to economic man.

The obvious choice of module, because of its summary properties as well as the presumptive centrality of value orientations, was the moral mode of the normative system. Given the dimensions descriptive of that aspect of the model, the following typology seemed to provide both plausibility and utility:

Types of Political Men
in terms of moral mode of norm system (i.e., goal definition)

Maximizers

particularistic	universalistic	
Social Man	Religious Man	other orientation
Economic Man	Principled Man	self orientation

Illustratively, in terms of the most familiar type—the economic—this provides for goal definition in terms of (1) maximization (2) of self-interest, which is defined (3) in material or physical terms. Within the parameters of an uncertain universe, imperfect information, and the individual capacity to err, it is assumed he pursues these goals in a rational manner, as that term is typically used by current theorists.[157] The other three types are similarly *rational,* but their goals are defined differently: the social type seeking other-oriented, particularistic goals; the religious type—other-oriented, abstract goals; and the principled type—self-oriented, abstract goals. All are defined as maximizers of their goals, but their payoffs may be in cash, love, salvation or principle, depending on the type involved.

While no claims need be made that the typology is either comprehensive or adequate to all situations, it does provide for some common political types, and does suggest affinities and hostilities between the types: the social and religious types sharing an "other" orientation, for instance; the social and principled types being opposed on both dimensions, as are the economic and religious.[158] It is perhaps unnecessary here to reiterate that all are political—that is, all are designed to capture behavior types found in the situations commonly recognized as politics. Each is of interest here only in that aspect, and the description will not include treatment of the type as it might be of interest in other contexts.[159]

Economic Man

Economic Man [160] is, in the present typology, the same as that model currently used under the name of rational or economic man, since conceptual clarity hardly would be served if another meaning were to be substituted. He is practical, interested in the utility of goods for his own self-preservation; in general, his "payoffs" must be in tangible, immediate terms. He may be described in somewhat villainous terms, as in Rousseau's condemnation of "the man who first fenced the common land" and induced men to accept their chains; or in more admiring terms as a sensible, nonideological yeoman figure who is the solid enduring base of the middle-class polity.[161] Since Economic Man is used so widely as the equivalent of political man, it should be clearly stated here that, by definition, the type we intend to describe as economic is not interested in any abstract sort of power or domination but only in hard goods—which may be land, gold, or cattle, depending on the societal value designations.

In addition to the description in terms of moral norms that is used to create the type, Economic Man's cognitive norms may be postulated as (1) skepticism (2) self-validation, and (3) particularism. In order, that is, to ensure his "safety" from deception, this individual maintains a general attitude of disbelief; when he does believe something, it will be that which he has "seen with his own eyes" and not that he is told by some authority. The parameters of his cognitive world are, thirdly, in practical terms: abstractions do not interest him; and theories (and theorists) are inimical to his thinking.[162] Economic Man may be further described in terms of his cognitive beliefs. His beliefs about man are, hypothetically (1) that man is disciplined, pleasure being seen as positively dangerous;[163] and (2) self-oriented, any form of altruism being inconceivable to Economic Man. On the third dimension, two subtypes can be usefully distinguished: Economic Man$_1$ who defines men in particularistic terms and is thus parochial in orientation, whatever society he is part of (and, in difficult times, whose life may be classically "nasty, brutish and short"); and Economic Man$_2$ who, by his perception of man in abstract terms, is capable of the Hobbesian leap in which he progresses from raw nature to the Leviathan, for purely self-interested reasons.[164]

Social Man

Social Man, the second of the types here under consideration, has been defined previously in terms of a moral norm pattern of (1) maximizing (2) other-oriented, (3) physical gratifications: that is, he values humanity and human love. Because he values people as "ends in themselves," in a choice situation Social Man will prefer mercy to justice, cooperation to conflict, and peace to war. He is a personalizer of abstractions, a subjectivist; he finds theory cold, and finds men of principle bloodless; cognitively, his norms are (1) belief, (2) self-validated, in (3) the particular immediate reality. In terms of the remaining aspect of the norm system, the expressive or stylistic, one may postulate Social Man warm and open, group-oriented, and profuse or rich in manner and style. This stylistic aspect is, however, secondary; the critical question in defining Social Man is his position on the *goal* norms of "other" orientation and particularistic definition.

When the definitional process is expanded into the cognitive *belief* system, two familiar types can be distinguished. Social Man will make his definition of man in terms of freedom and "other" orientation. The third dimension suggests the two distinguishable subtypes: (1) Definition of men in terms of physical, particularistic criteria such as family, race, and religion; this subtype might be called tribal man, or, under certain conditions, the bigot. (2) If definitions are made in universalistic terms, the subtype of Social Man will resemble natural man as described by Rousseau or Montesquieu: harmless, sociable, and open.

Religious Man

Religious Man,[165] the third variation on patterns of moral norms, is distinguished by his "other" orientation and universalistic or abstract form of definition. By the former dimension, it may be noted, he has a resemblance to the social type; by the latter, with the principled type. Religious Man too is common to political life: he is the individual who seeks salvation in something outside himself, through unity with some relatively abstract "other," be that a god or a political grouping. He may resemble Hoffer's "man of fanatical faith who is ready to scarifice his life for a holy cause,"[166] or, since one man's fanatic is another man's saviour, Religious Man may be described as a charismatic leader (or follower); or generally, any variety of idealistic revolutionary.[167]

In terms of cognitive orientation, one may postulate a descriptive configuration of (1) belief, (2) other-validation, and (3) universalistic definitions of reality. This cognitive pattern, while of course hypothetical, raises some interesting suggestions concerning the genesis of political extremists within democratic political systems: if, as Lane suggests, a stubborn (and courageous) skepticism is useful for maintaining the governmental forms involved, then it may be that this cognitive belief position is exactly what generates the extremist tendency.[168] Notably, Religious Man is the converse of Economic Man, in the present typology.

Once again we may amplify the parameters of Religious Man by considering his cognitive and preferential beliefs concerning man. It seems probable that the Religious Man is characterized by a sharp distinction between the two belief systems as follows: man is *perceived* as disciplined, alone, and particularistically defined; he would rather be free, without loneliness, and be universalistically defined. The first two points stand clearly enough; the third perhaps needs illustration. The pattern has been often recognized: the outcast group, defined generally on racial or cryptoracial grounds, that seizes upon a new religion that "rises above" such distinctions. That this universalism may change into a new particularism (involving a shift to the bigot type of Social Man) does not vitiate the religious quality of the process: few revolutions escape the devouring of at least some of their children before reaction sets in.

Principled Man

The final member of the typology suggested by the dimensional model is Principled Man, one who sets as his moral norm pattern the (1) maximization of (3) universalistic goals for (2) self-oriented [169] reasons. That is, Principled Man gives first priority to abstract rules; he may be called a legalist, a moralist, or—as we shall suggest—a politician. The first distinction into subtypes involves the cognitive norm system. One variety may be described as (1) believer, (2) other-validation, and (3) universalistic; this combination produces legalists and moralists. [170] The second variety of Principled Man is defined by its cognitive-norm set of (1) skepticism, (2) self-validation, and (3) particularism; it closely resembles Spranger's political type, that type interested in power, influence, and renown.

Principled Man$_1$ is a type that needs little introduction; it could encompass the follower of Kant's categorical imperative, the congressman who asks not "will it work?" but rather "is it constitutional?" and the (perhaps empirically rare) administrator who strives to be a neutral tool of his orders or his superiors. [171]

Principled Man$_2$—old "machtmensch"—is an infamous type included here with some reluctance. Power, as the discipline keeps telling itself, is evasive, illusive, and impossible of definition; yet these arguments have not eliminated the term. Political Man is included here on utilitarian grounds: [172] there are behavioral patterns not easily explained by any of the other types, including paradigmatic Economic Man. Such behaviors might include the man who lends money solely to *indebt* the borrower to him, the administrator who evaluates every proposal solely with respect to its impact on his perquisites, the businessman who sinks funds in a venture he knows will cost him heavily in cash terms but will nonetheless bring him prestige. Until these and similar actions can be explained in other terms, provision must be made for Political Man. By way of summary, the types may be described as in Figure 3.

SUMMARY

Working from the premise that the basic political fact is man, and that political science can develop as an empirical science only by recognizing this human base, we have argued that:

(1) Ethically it is acceptable to theorize about man because he is so complex he will elude our best efforts for generations to come;

(2) The refusal to build a political psychology on systematic empirical grounds will frustrate any progress toward middle-range theory—so essential to comparative politics;

(3) The model of economic man, like all single-factor explanations, is too narrow for the geographic variety the discipline must encompass;

(4) There is a coherence in the psychologically oriented research, but much confusion and wasted effort also.

	Particularism	Universalism

Other	**000 Social Man**
	
	Values:
	  Altruism, mercy, tolerance of frailty, loyalty, love, humanity
	
	Cognitive Norms:
	  Belief/self/particularism
	
	Cognitive Beliefs (man):
	  Gratifying/other-orientation and if particularistic, then tribal/bigot; if universalistic, then natural man
		001 Religious Man
		
		Values:
		  Purity, idealism, salvation, refusal to compromise, unity
		
		Cognitive Norms:
		  Belief/other/universalism

Self	**010 Economic Man**
	
	Values:
	  Wealth, utility, practicality, success, self-preservation
	
	Cognitive Norms:
	  Skeptic/self/particularism
	
	Cognitive Beliefs (man):
	  Discipline/self and if particularistic, then narrowly self-interested; if universalistic, then long-range capability
		011 Principled Man
		
		MORALIST/LEGALIST
		Values:
		  Law, equity, duty, rectitude
		
		Cognitive Norms:
		  Belief/other/universalism
		
		POLITICAL
		Values:
		  Power, face, influence, domination
		
		Cognitive Norms:
		  Skeptic/self/particularism

Figure 3: Summary Typology Based on Moral Mode of Normative System Using Second Two Dimensions (all are maximizers on first dimension)

With a constructive approach to political theory, which sees it as an integral part of science, a model of political man has been developed. This model provides for a core belief system of attitudes concerning man, society, tradition, and the physical world; a parallel system of preferences with respect to the four objects; and a normative system encompassing epistemological, stylistic, and moral modes of evaluation. On the latter mode, a preliminary typology has been constructed, adding to economic man three companion models—social, religious, and principled men. In each case, the main type has been ramified into some of its more obvious subtypes through the use of the complementary modules.

Starting thus from the Platonic premise that "men differ" we have attempted to show, within the available empirical research, what the contemporary answer has been; and within the context of that demonstration, to clarify the parameters of the investigation.

NOTES

1. The debate over the "real" meaning of the classics is not one we wish to enter; here the position is taken that if a simple, common-sense interpretation can be found, there is no intrinsic objection to it. In this view, the author of the Platonic dialogs is taken to be an empirical theorist. For part of the debate over politics and sophistry see Plato's Gorgias (Helmbold, 1952).

2. The literature is extensive with boundaries as variable as human definition. Perhaps the most useful review of contemporary work is Greenstein (1969) and especially Lerner (1969: 154-184). Works germinal to the present research include: Lane (1962); Verba (1965); Lasswell (1962); Levi-Strauss (1967); Northrop (1960); Rokeach (1960); Deutsch (1963); Homans (1950).

3. What is "concrete" and what "abstract" is of course another ancient battleground; the intent here is to exclude those approaches that define the "essence" of political science to be in such evasive notions as "sovereignty" or "power." If these terms have meaning, it is only in their aspect as qualities of human attitudes and behavior; in this aspect they have been included in the present model (see Part V).

4. Sartori's critique (1969) and prescriptive analysis (1970) are exemplary discussions of this problem.

5. Instances of the various oddities into which personal or disciplinary bias has led hardly need be given; illustrative is the graduate student who after a study of economic development problems in Latin America recommended that since the norm of "machismo" was dysfunctional for modern economic practices, it should be given up. Unfortunately, such naivete is not exclusive to graduate students.

6. Alker's alternatives (1965: 33-34), which still leave open the basic question of what values exist in a particular context, are the democratic $e_i = \bar{v}$ (the mean value) or the proportional $e_i = km_i$ (k is a constant of proportion and m is a variable of merit). That the model so clearly raises these questions is to its credit; that so little attempt has been made toward answering them is unfortunate. The economic perspective does not preclude a broader metric of "utiles" (see Black, 1972: 145-146), although this has been generally overlooked.

7. What Plato meant, plausibly, may but be that one type of people is better at growing potatoes, and another at governing; since both these functions are necessary to the state, they are equally worthy. The Greek use of the term "arete" suggests this interpretation. (Cf. Sabine, 1937: 45-50).

8. Despite the prevalence of "systems theory," there are few attempts at theoretical clarification intended to bridge the area between this highly generalized theory and the real world of behavior. A classic exception is Morton Kaplan's definition of six intra-systemic "states" and their maintenance and transformation rules (Kaplan, 1957: 21-53). The original and by now historic call for middle-range theory was Macridis (1955); a recent discussion of the comparative problem is Lijphart (1971).

9. The investigator into the numerous social disciplines, subdisciplines, cross-disciplines and quasi-disciplines that converge on the question of political man finds a plethora of material, much of it at one or the other methodological extreme. Illustrative general compilations include: Borgatta and Lambert (1968); Clausen (1968); Hsu (1961); Bert Kaplan (1961); Lindzey and Aronson (1968). Collections of attitude scales from relevant fields present a wide and inchoate variety; see, inter

alia, Robinson, et al. (1968); Robinson and Shaver (1969); Shaw and Wright (1967). Few of the social sciences provide paradigms readily adaptable to political science. In the psychological fields the Freudian approach has suffered only mild revisions since its nineteenth-century formulation (see the useful discussion by Berkowitz, 1968: 52 esp., although the theory was even then untestable–in the sense of being open to rejection on empirical grounds. At the empirical end of the spectrum are the research-oriented "trait" and "attitude" studies where even advanced analytical techniques often fail to bring coherence to the data. (See, for instance, Cattell, 1946; and Eysenck, 1953. That factor analysis did lead to Eysenck's tough and tender-minded dimension was a hopeful, if atypical, piece of synthesis.) In anthropology similarly the "national character" school went its broad-gauge way, providing, at its best, useful insights into the bases of behavior; while the more methodologically concerned studies bogged down in the ambituities of cross-cultural Rorschach interpretation (see Hsu, 1961; and Kaplan, 1961, respectively). The sociological dilemma has been between whole-society analysis (see, e.g., Parsons 1951; and Klausner, 1967) and narrow, empirical treatments of role traits and socialization patterns. That political science has in its eclecticism acquired these methodological problems wholesale is clear from two recent surveys: Greenstein (1969) and Siegel (1970). Lasswell's 40-year-old plea that the discipline "ascertain the traits with which the various individuals [politicians, judges, agitators] *begin* to practice their role in society," so that a "rigorous audit" of the effects of institutions and roles can be made, remains unanswered (quoted in Greenstein, 1969: 151 and 153). The point is devastating: at no point, be it man's political predispositions, his roles, or his adult personality and its political ramifications for societal institutions, at no point have we even a primitive conceptual model for describing what we are talking about. So, to suggest one particularly unfortunate case, "political socialization" studies are reduced to the trivial definitions of *political,* rather than asking what types of *citizens* are possible? what sorts of *situations* produce them? and so on. Surely political science will not reassert its master-science prerogative unless it is willing to ask questions, the answers to which have implications.

10. This approach is exemplified in Downs (1957) and in Buchanan and Tullock (1962); the more recent works in political economy do not always maintain their rigorous microanalytic level. Thrasymachus' argument is of course found in *The Republic;* and is reevaluated in Dahrendorf (1968: 129-150).

11. Buchanan and Tullock (1962) demonstrate that the analysis can be carried to the constitutional level; compare Shubik (1964: 41-42) where a prison system that is self-policing under economic assumptions concerning man would be worthless if one altruist could be found.

12. We do not intend to slight the ethical concern here; only to suggest that at this point in time and science, the citizen is sufficiently protected by the ignorance of those who study him. Some more systematic outrage is occasionally necessary (Horowitz, 1967).

13. Hume's plaint (1961: 229) that he could never find a "self," only perceptions and thoughts, is characteristic.

14. Sartori's discussion (1970) of this process and the methodological strictures on it are extremely useful.

15. The general exception is *The Civic Culture* (Almond and Verba, 1963), but progress along this path has been hampered by the same barrier, or hiatus, that has arrested the development of theoretic substance in American surveying–the failure of

middle-range analytic frameworks. In the large and theoretically interesting range between the pollster's trivia and the psychoanalyst's couch we have few if any guidelines.

16. Two rare, if relatively recent, exceptions are McKinney (1966) and Stinchcombe (1968).

17. Whatever other uses one may envision for the constructs of the major political theorists, their utility as research guides need not be slighted. That such utilization may require close analysis, as illustrated by Robert Dahl's treatment of Madison (1956: ch. 1) and a constructive approach tolerant of the theorist's ambiguity (Kaplan, 1964: 65-68 esp.), should not prevent the use of a good idea. The notion that any theory means what its author "meant"—no more and no less—is clearly dysfunctional.

18. The formulation implies that the questions must be operationally answerable; suitable, that is, for relatively direct conversion into testable hypotheses. The motivation behind the exercise is the development of categories suitable for computer tabulation; for evidence of the paucity of theory useable in this area see the discussion of extant models in Loehlin (1968). That social science simulations attain much of their utility in precisely this area of "forced" theory building is noted frequently by practitioners. For a compelling argument that constructed types can serve as the link between theory and empirical research see McKinney (1966: 38-39): "The constructed type can perform the important service of functioning as a bridge between systematic substantive theory and relatively unstructured empirical data. As a conceptual device, the constructed type represents an attempt to advance concept formation in the social sciences from the stage of description and 'empirical generalization' to the construction of theoretical systems."

19. As J. H. Woodger (1939: 75) states: "... the role of definition is not primarily to provide new information. They might rather be said to be the receptacles of present information with the aid of which such information is tested."

20. See the discussion in Chapter I, Background, on politics as "simplifier."

21. The inquiring psychologist, despite his American empirical bias, is likely to be impressed by the heroic constructs of the Geisteswissenschaften schools (see for an instance Spranger, 1966), but deterred by their philosophical baggage. It would seem somehow that both the simplistic trivia sometimes characteristic of pure empiricism and the monumental complexities reminiscent of the nineteenth century could be superseded.
nineteenth century could be superseded.

22. For an evaluation of the fourth point, the reader must be left to his own devices.

23. Compare Machiavelli's oddly Platonic trichotomy of (1) those who can think for themselves, (2) those who can understand when shown, and (3) those who can do neither. See, The Prince, Chapter XXII (Lerner, 1940: 86).

24. The style is associated with the contract theorists of the seventeenth and eighteenth centuries, but it can be traced to Plato's Laws (Taylor, 1960: III) and Seneca's Golden Age; cf. Sabine (1937: 78, 177-178). As a mode of analysis it appears to acquire greater importance in periods of transition, as in the work of the Renaissance Scholastics; see Copleston (1963: 167 ff.).

25. While the utility of this notion may be declining, we intend it in the approximate definition of Kuhn (1962); for a useful discussion of the controversy and question from a political viewpoint see Landau (1972: 43-77).

26. The natural science approach associated with the work of Lorenz (1966) is one of the more popular attempts toward the solution of this question, although of doubtful objectivity, as suggested by the reprinting of quotations from Lorenz's 1940 German publications in Eisenberg (1972: 124-125). The complexity of the findings concerning the "innate" vs. "learned" nature of birdsong is summarized in this excellent article: "Songsparrows, isolated from conspecifics and foster-reared by canaries, nonetheless acquire their own song. Yet meadowlarks, similarly isolated as fledglings, acquire the song of the particular foster species. . . . [T] he white-crowned sparrow . . . must hear the adult model of its song during a "sensitive period" of development in order to acquire it; nonetheless, if the fledgling white-crowned sparrow is simultaneously exposed to conspecifics and to two sympatric species, it 'learns' *only its own song.*"

27. Abelson and Carroll's (1965) Goldwater machine is an illustration of how useful this approach can be in the proper hands.

28. The pragmatic approach may be the refuge of the mediocre: Russell (1945: 123-124) clearly opts for the "sudden insight" in creativity; he is kind enough to retail William James' story of the man who comprehended the universe as a caveat to assuming that sudden insights are always accurate. Deutsch (1963: 100) also discusses the question. The approach taken in the current exercise is philosophically akin to the position of Stinchcombe (1968: 3): That "theory ought to create the capacity to invent explanations."

29. This is what Kaplan (1964: 79, italics original) calls the corollary to his central principle of the autonomy of inquiry, the *autonomy of the conceptual base:* "A scientist *may* use whatever concepts he *can* use, whatever ones he finds useful in fact. The restriction to which he is subject is only that what he says be capable of being checked by experience."

30. This analysis only partly reflects Deutsch's own interpretation of his intellectual task; compare Deutsch (1963: x-xi). His approach to systems theory seems to bring it closer to the original systems theory of Von Bertalanffy than to the varieties common to political science; a useful discussion is found in Young (1968: ch. 2). See also Wiener (1948) and Von Neumann (1958).

31. Laswell and Kaplan (1950). The work was completed in 1945 (see their "Preface," p. vi), making it the earliest of the sources here under discussion (Parsons and Shils and their colleagues began work in 1949-1950; Parsons and Shils, 1951: v). The representation here is intended to organize the works around the conceptual problem, not trace intellectual history.

32. Quotations are from *Power and Society* (Lasswell and Kaplan, 1950); references are given in parentheses.

33. The basic presentation is in Part II, ch. 1 "Categories of the Orientation and Organization of Action," (Parsons and Shils, 1951: 53-109).

34. The most notable case was of course Parsons' own shift from "Model I" to "Model II"; see Dubin (1960) and Parsons' rejoinder (Parsons, 1960). The so-called "economic" theorists did maintain the microanalytic approach, but such careful works as Buchanan and Tullock (1962) failed of widespread recognition within political science.

35. "(The habit [of affectivity] implies that in perhaps a majority of the situations an attitude of affectivity will apply, but no relationship between human beings can remain always on the affectivity level—this, perhaps, is what we mean by saying 'we are not beasts.')" (Parsons and Shils, 1951: 89).

36. The deductive necessity of the pattern variables (Parsons and Shils, 1951: 76 ff.) is here considered irrelevant; that they summarized a strain of conceptual thought within the behavioral sciences and have continued to interest both theoreticians and empiricists is sufficient. Their utility in the present work was a function of the abstraction level that allowed application at four levels; concrete action, habits of decision (personality), role definition, and value standards (Parsons and Shils, 1951: 78).

37. The reduction to three is here justified only by Occam's principle; it does however fit with the initial presentation of the pattern variable model, which distinguished these three as primary (Parsons and Shils, 1951: 84). Certain questions concerning the self-collectivity dichotomy seem less difficult in the political context as here defined.

38. The binary numbering is the outcome of coding each of the three dimensions to a column; affectivity, other-orientation and particularism are coded 0; the alternate pole in each case is coded 1 (the direction is of course *gemeinschaft-gesellschaft*).

39. Operationally it is not as complex as it might appear: (1) not all elements need be used in a single analysis, as we discuss later in the text; and (2) even if *all* elements are used, summary for a single individual would require only 11 arabic digits.

40. The obvious but frequently ignored point is made by McKinney (1966: 144): "[A] systemic structural analysis is a prerequisite for anything approximating a compelling analysis of change." For discussion of the functional aspects of belief systems in social terms see Lane (1969); and in relation to internal concerns, Rokeach (1960); and Festinger (1957). The *gestalt* school in general is discussed in Meehan (1967: 205 ff.). One of the few discussions of adult learning patterns is Brim (1968: 182-226).

41. The term is that used in the "general theory of action"; there are of course far more than we discuss here.

42. While the extreme relativism implied seems to be a desirable corrective to the "civilized bias" common to Western investigators (see Levi-Strauss, 1966), we do not suggest that all world views are equally efficacious. *Ceteris paribus,* better bombs are more apt to be successful in winning a war than are libation offerings to deities; the qualified form of this assertion should be clear.

43. This definition of objects is common to the original presentation of action theory (Kluckhohn, 1951: 410) and is adopted in the specifically political redefinition of Verba (1965: 521-522).

44. The (hypothetically) nonrandom distribution of the nonmodal types within each society would be a primary object of empirical study.

45. Furthermore, any one individual may have during any time period a variety of roles, some of which will involve different dimensional patterns. He may, that is, in his (1) father role, couch his cognitive beliefs about man in terms of "restraint," "community" and particularism (e.g., loyalty to the family); while in his (2) work role, he may cast those same beliefs in terms of gratification (assuming he enjoys his job), individualism, and universalistic criteria of definition. The point is not the particular orientations described, but the fact that an individual *could* (and probably will) have a different pattern on each of several roles simultaneously.

46. Discussion of cognitive beliefs concerning the definition of man tends to raise the reader's rejection of some of the polar possibilities on moral or ethical grounds. Second thoughts or a course in anthropology usually cure this bias. At any

rate, the following discussion assumes that for purposes of analysis, the puritan ethic of restraint and the perhaps more ancient norm of *carpe diem* are equally plausible—and moral.

47. Perhaps the most useful recent treatment of the problem of "will" is Deutsch (1963: 105-107).

48. Despite Aristotle, many "outsiders" are neither beasts or gods, but simply outsiders. We do not suggest here as a possible choice *complete* solitude, which would be a deviant situation. For a discussion of some relevant empirical work (on self-sufficiency vs. gregariousness and independence) see Cattell (1946: 361-362).

49. This is similar but not equivalent to the moral norm (infra) distinguishing "greater love hath no man . . ." from "sauve-qui-peut." There is no unnecessary tautology.

50. The ease and "self-evidence" of operational definition is probably a good criterion of the level of abstraction; if observers tend to disagree on the definition, the concept *tends* toward higher abstraction; this could be put in quantitative terms.

51. This dimension is intended as broader than, but including the pattern variable, ascription-achievement (see Parsons and Shils, 1951: 57, 82-83).

52. As noted above, the basic module may be used more than once for a single individual, if necessary to the complete description of his several role orientations.

53. The product of 2^3: the three dichotomous dimensions here under discussion. This is not to be confused with the broad-gauge typology in Part IV.

54. One's view here is apparently a function of the surrounding circumstances; Hobbes and Burke may be illustrative.

55. This definition apparently is similar to that of the same dimension under 1-i, but is distinguishable on the grounds that it is possible to have two different positions. One may be a Polish-American Catholic and one may make that criterion one's self-definition as well as the rule for friendship, marriage, etc., and yet be aware that the whole society is structured, at least in parts, on nonparticularistic lines. This involves only cognition, "what *is* the case," not preferences which the model treats separately under (2) below.

56. An operational index of the nongratifying pole, the "cruel world" index, is found in Sniderman and Citrin (1971: 407): "statements that describe the world as an unhappy, threatening place in which true values cannot be preserved." While there is a social-human flavor to this world, it clearly implies the natural world, and thus fits the present dimension.

57. This bias should not occur in the present case because, inter alia, the dimension is used in conjunction with two others.

58. It of course is possible for man in a given empirical situation to perceive a government as an object in this sense; and the type chosen here by any given individual might be compared with government as society or as tradition to clarify the multiple aspects of the political realm.

59. We do not intend to denote by tradition the political tradition, which generally connotes only institutions; the relevant tradition here is wider than that, as is clear from the description, but narrower than the total culture studied by the anthropologist; and, of course, narrower than political man in total model definition.

60. Again, this is not the Parsonian achievement-ascription dimension, which is but a special case of it.

61. On this general approach see Easton (1965), esp. Part III, "The Input of Support" (153-243).

62. Some process similar to this would undoubtedly explain adult socialization patterns (see Brim, 1968), where the behavior is less explicable in terms of conflict resolution between varying roles, but rather involves an active attempt by ego to fulfill some postulated goal. That sort of positive goal would be described in terms of the appreciative belief system.

63. It is perhaps similar to what Deutsch means by consciousness, that is, the system's capacity to control its own goal-seeking activity (see Deutsch, 1963: 98-109 "Consciousness and Will as Patterns of Communication Flow").

64. The most abstract level, i.e., epistemology (see Mannheim, n.d.: 13ff).

65. The criterion used is still "utility."

66. The polarity is nicely illustrated between the "true believer" described by Hofer (1951) and Boorstin's American "genius" with his empty sanctum sanctorum (1953: x).

67. As on the previous dimension, these distinctions are not absolute: independent thinkers are apt to be discontent if *no* colleagues rally to their discoveries. One of the earliest statements of the situation is Plato's *Crito* where Socrates rejects mass opinion as a criterion of action (Jowett, 1942: 69). But polar modalities can be discerned; compare the regnant empiricist paradigm to the statement by Levi-Strauss, admittedly somewhat ambiguous, that follows; "Meaning is not decreed; if it is not everywhere, it is nowhere" (1963: 91).

68. The distinction is not of course between theory and method, but between science as the study of and belief in predictable regularities or the search for laws and the exact reportorial detail of the case study, where no generalizations are made.

69. Socialization, or physical differences in addition to intelligence, also may be at work in forming this orientation. Sex differences are illustrative: cf. the often noted modal differences in male-female classroom behavior.

70. This cognitive search problem is part of that described by Fromm (1941), and by Dostoevski's (1957) *Grand Inquisitor*. Unless there is a high tolerance for cognitive ambiguity, the other-oriented skeptic presumably shifts to the believer pole, though socially supported nihilism may be an alternative.

71. The view that it is immoral to study man is rather a function of the substantive belief systems relating to the definition of man, society, and the object world.

72. We assume here an underlying Benthamite idea of all men seeking "pleasure" of some form; it is the nature of that form that is the concern of the model. The assumption itself may be considered as a simplifying one, common to most such discussions, and does not preclude the ascetic response.

73. That these sorts of choices, though apparently elusive, can be operationally tested is shown by Rokeach (1968: 156-178).

74. Rokeach's work suggests an illustration: the end-value "freedom," which, as he noted, may mean quite different things to differently situated persons. On this dimension, the difference would be between the freedom of some member of a socially stigmatized group, which would tend to mean his own personal (particularistic) freedom, and the freedom valued by some individual who holds it up as a broadly applicable norm, distinct from his own objective position. Mannheim's comparison of the meaning of freedom to a nineteenth-century German conservative (an estate's right to live according to its privileges) and to the romantic-conservative-Protestant (the individual's right to live according to his own personality) is

analogous: the former being particularistic, clear; the latter universalistic, vague (in implication). (See Mannheim, n.d.: 273)

75. The classic case is Adorno et al. (1950); (see, of course, Christie and Jahoda, 1954). We do not intend to denigrate either the particular work, or the inevitable incursions of subjectivity; only to suggest the necessity for constant reevaluation.

76. Major reference works cited in the following discussion include: Robinson et al. (1968); Robinson and Shaver (1969); Miller (1970); Shaw and Wright (1967); Bonjean et al. (1967).

77. A major research-oriented use of the concept appears in Herbert McCloskey's Political Affiliations and Beliefs project: relevant articles include di Palma and McCloskey (1970: 1054-1073); and McCloskey and Schaar (1960: 14-40). An early scale of ego strength is Barron (1953: 327-333) included in Robinson and Shaver (1969: 130-134); conceived broadly to cover physical condition, psychasthenia, seclusiveness, religious and moral attitudes, sense of reality, phobias, anxieties, and personal adequacy. A useful discussion of the general area of ego *defense* is McGuire (1968: 136-314, esp. 157-160). The contrasting schools of tension-reduction and developmental theorists are outlined usefully in Zigler and Child (1968): 450-589, esp. 468-473).

78. Sniderman and Citrin (1971: 410-417, esp. 405) redefine self-esteem into three dimensions, relating to personal unworthiness, social competence, and social inferiority. Similar is Coopersmith's 1967 "self-esteem inventory," involving one's perception of self as capable, significant, successful, and worthy; see Robinson and Shaver (1969: 126-129). "Self-confidence" is used by McCloskey and Schaar (1965); "Competence" in the studies of the Survey Research Center is summarized in Robinson et al. (1968: 655-660) where it involves questions about one's ability to carry out plans, sureness about life, and expectation of more good than bad luck. Of the many scales developed to test self-esteem, Robinson and Shaver note that few are used more than once (1969: 45).

79. The situational aspect of self-esteem is nicely illustrated in the comparison of the star athlete at a scholarly conference and the scholar in the locker room in Marlowe and Gergen (1968: 590-665, 644-645).

80. Related conceptually here are the following: "initiative," defined by the Opinion Research Corporation (Robinson et al., 1968: 159-160), is operationally equivalent to competence; as is "issue familiarity" after the addition of certain stylistic components involving "willingness to express" opinions (Campbell et al., 1964: 171-176). "Life satisfaction" (McCloskey and Schaar, 1965) and "status frustration," and the frequent optimism-pessimism dimension all appear to be explicable functionally in terms of the individual's finding himself in a social, actual, and traditional context that provides at least some congruence and gratification.

81. When broken down to operational level, achievement tends to diffuse into other constructs. For instance, Kahl's "generalized motivation to excell" is closely related to the modernism syndrome, including trust, activism, occupational primacy, and attitudes towards relatives; the scale is described in Miller (1970: 327-329). One way of producing it is the Calvinist motivation discussed below.

82. The concept was developed by Murray (1938); the quotation is from Sniderman and Citrin (1971: 407).

83. For instance, Zigler and Child (1968: 526), report on an empirical study of under- and overcontrolling children in which the former respond aggressively to frustration, the latter adapt. Similarly, on a power-need vs. affection-need dimension,

the former react more aggressively than the latter to frustration (see also the discussion of aggression below.)

84. Except of course for the psychobiographical literature.

85. The suggestion of "balance" in patterns raises some of the most serious questions. While it might seem simpler to eliminate such terms, the substantive questions would remain; all we argue here, therefore, is that the pattern model provides a possible means of precise description that will make it feasible to investigate such notions as balance.

86. These would be "if-then" propositions rather than outright policy statements. If, for example, you seek a happy populace, patterns x and y appear to have a low association with anxiety and can be recommended; if you seek a productive populace, patterns p and q are associated with diligence and anxiety. Such an approach raises sharply the question of "functional for whom?"

87. Dogmatism is here used as developed by Rokeach (1960). The strongmindedness scale has been used in various Survey Research Center studies; it involves opinion flexibility, opinion strength, and changeability in arguments. (See summary in Robinson et al., 1968: 650-661; it is said to have had "only limited analytic success.")

88. Thomas and Znaniecki's (1965) "bohemian" man is exceptional; defined simply as unformed, adaptable, and inconsistent.

89. The other aspects are discussed under their appropriate headings. The substantive beliefs mentioned include attitudes about the "friendliness" of the world, discussed here as cognitive beliefs about man and the object world (see, for instance, "faith in people," "optimism," "cruel world," "cynicism," among others). The time perspective would seem to involve a combination of cognitive beliefs about man (whether he disciplines himself toward some *future* goal), and moral norms ("maximizers" that are typically future oriented).

90. The question of intensity presently is not provided for in the model. Largely upon an impetus supplied by Rokeach's work, it was the assumption that with the *adult* individual, *all* the beliefs and norms would be of sufficient intensity to qualify them as "primitive," that is, of central importance and resistant to quick changes. However, since even these beliefs are expected to change under sufficient pressure, it would be desirable at some point to be able to measure the subjective intensity with which beliefs are held; this easily could be accomodated by allowing for Thurstone type scale responses rather than the dichotomous approach probably for early stages of testing. See Rokeach (1968: ch. 1, "The Orgainzation and Modification of Beliefs").

91. I.e., within the Deutschian context.

92. The authoritarian concept is discussed below.

93. The concept originated with Frenkel-Brunswik (1949a: 295-306; 1949b: 108-143). A review of its utilization is in Robinson and Shaver (1969: 317-328). For Lane's discussion see (1964: 94ff.).

94. Cognitively, two patterns may produce tolerance of ambiguity: the true tolerant, who is skeptic/practical/self-reliant and the socialized tolerant, who is believer/theoretic/group-oriented, acquiring his perhaps slightly uncomfortable tolerance through education; the latter clearly seems closer to Lane's type (1962: 94ff.).

95. Three other cognitive concepts may be mentioned here: intellectuality and mysticism, used by McCloskey and Schaar (1965: 26), and the tough- and tender-minded dimension (Eysenck, 1953: 2d ed. 1960: 366 ff.). Intellectuality is in

fact a misnomer for an orientation toward cultural activities; in the present model, it would be a choice of the theoretic pole, either through belief or skepticism. Mysticism would fall on the believer pole of the first dimension combined with adherence to self-oriented validation of truths. The frequently pejorative definition of mysticism—as belief in spiritualism, necromancy, astrology, portents: generally as belief in magical rather than scientific explanations—is a third-dimensional choice of particularism over universalism in the module involving cognitive beliefs concerning the real world. Types of mysticism could be defined precisely through utilization of the model to clarity subtypes. Nature mystics, for example, would be defined by their attitude toward the natural world (cf. the discussion in Chapter III, Cognitive Belief—concerning the physical world). The tough-tender dimension (similar to the Jungian introvert-extrovert distinction, (Eysenck, 1953: 385), opposes the practical-materialistic-direct action type to the theoretical-idealistic-thinker or believer. Clearly these categories relate directly to the dimensions provided by the present model.

Related is the problem of egalitarianism vs. elitism; cf. the operationally defined index used by Sniderman and Citrin, 1971: 410: "Disposition to derogate man's intelligence and political capacity and a willingness to see some men as intrinsically superior, of a 'finer breed' than others." Only some vehicle such as we have here attempted to provide for the *precise* description of the "ideal" type (for a given individual) can save this sort of analysis from assuming everyone recognizes the same types of superiority, which is clearly false—illustrated by the saying: "we are the people our parents warned us against."

97. The discussion ranges from classic political theory to modern ethology. The quotation is from Hobbes (1958: 107).

98. On these latter two concepts, a note is in order concerning the odd bias inherent in their usage. Associated with authoritarianism research, little thought has been given to the possibility that the aesthete, for instance, may be equally intolerant or contemptuous, but of different qualities which he does, however, term weakness. By recognizing these supposedly partial constructs as general ones, new research possibilities are opened.

99. See the chapter on the Danzigs (Laing and Esterson, 1970: 109-130). A simple case that is a direct product of the types of persons involved, rather than the peculiarities of the situation, might be either: (a) the other-oriented pleasure seeker who wishes to associate with a self-oriented individual and is refused, or (b) the self-oriented, goal-directed individual who needs the help of the pleasure-seeker and finds him disinclined to work.

100. The explanation thus avoids the premature closure of questions concerning innate aggressiveness.

101. Mason suggests that the Negro in colonial situations had three response options, "acceptance, avoidance, aggression" (1970:45).

102. See discussion of Calvinism below.

103. Q.v. above.

104. We are not suggesting that all people who do these things are reacting to (or sublimating, in the Freudian sense) aggressive tendencies. One form of aggression that may be seen as more narrowly political would be criminal behavior—either at the individual or the system level; again the model provides some basis for discriminating *various* criminal patterns instead of the overaggregated approach that treats all deviance as essentially similar. Among the types one might delineate abstractly would be (1) the individual strongly disciplined by a tradition or society that simultaneously

defines him as an outcast; with no reason for allegiance, he easily turns to a self-definition that emphasizes gratification; if this is for self, he may become a petty criminal; if for others, he may become a Robin Hood. (2) Another type may be the individual with maximizing goals and a skeptical attitude toward common moral maxims who accepts a success-oriented tradition and proceeds toward that goal by swindling, bribery and other such means. Without attempting to make any fuller delineation here, the point may be summarized: the general concept of aggression, as well as the criminal subtype thereof, neither can be defined nor used with any precision unless it is recognized as a complex phenomenon and unless some formal mode of explicating its genesis and prognosis is provided. If, that is, we attempt to deal with the various types under one aggregated rubric, the search for empirical correlations will be hindered severely.

105. Utilized in empirical studies since the 1930s; see summary listing in Bonjean et al. (1967: 273-275).

106. The game-theoretic term is used here intentionally; one of the possible products of the model would be a psychologically broader definition of this aspect.

107. To avoid misinterpretation, it should be emphasized that we are making no judgment of intrinsic worth here; the latter individual is perhaps more pleasant in personality and probably happier, but he is unlikely, in most contexts, to dominate.

108. Cf. note 99.

109. While this point epistemologically is touchy, it may be illustrated as follows: if I believe in rain gods, and you are a trained meteorologist, your success in predicting rain is apt to be greater.

110. Cf. Machiavelli's discussion of cyclicality, The Discourses Book I, Chapter 2. Each form of government degenerates because the moderation of the initiators gives way to excess in the next generation.

111. We include faith in trust, although the former may be more preferential than cognitive. McCloskey uses faith (1967). The SRC scale is included in Robinson et al. (1968: 662).

112. The series was dropped after 1964; see Robinson et al. (1968: 653).

113. The discussion includes by implication the obverse attitude: misanthropy, cynicism, and machiavellianism. Misanthropy is defined by McCloskey (1967: 66) as involving such statements as "you have to be choosy about picking friends," "I distrust people who try to be different from most of us"; Agger, Goldstein and Pearl (Robinson et al., 1968: 479-481) define cynicism, both personal and political, in terms of distrust and contempt; the Christie Mach scale adds to this certain beliefs concerning tactics (Robinson and Shaver, 1969: 506-516).

114. It is notable that the fairness question received the highest positive response in the 1964 survey (Robinson et al., 1968: 653).

115. Its broader implications are discussed under authoritarianism below.

116. Adorno et al. (1960: 104); the concept was originally the E Scale (Ch. IV).

117. Cf. Rokeach (1968), Ch. 3, "Race and Shared Belief as Factors in Social Choice," on the dominance of ideology over particularistic criteria of social choice.

118. This also might reveal some uninvestigated affinities between apparently unrelated groups; pro-Semitism among traditional Yankees, for instance.

119. The Litt "political chauvinism" scale is representative: agreement with statements glorifying the American political system, and Americans in general, as the "best." See scale and references in Robinson and Shaver (1969: 475-478).

120. If the attitude is a direct function of the socialization process, absorbed

without skepticism, chauvinism is equivalent formally to internationalism; the question is only to which traditions various social strata are exposed. Substantively, chauvinism is a choice of the particularistic definition of man (i.e., the third dimension of cognitive beliefs concerning man).

121. Among the operational approaches, which have at least the virtue of precision, one finds illustratively: Prothro and Grigg, "attitude towards democratic principles" of democracy, majority rule, minority rights (Robinson et al., 1968: 179-181); and McCloskey, "democratic and antidemocratic attitudes" relating to rules of game, free speech, equality, etc. (1967: 170-178). Dahl (1970) substantially amplifies his discussion of political man (ch. 6) and concludes with a dichotomous choice of "the democratic character" vs. the despotic alternative.

122. That More's hedonism was tempered by a concern for harmony and that Calvinism sought eschatological gratification is covered by the system of moral norms.

123. "All men" have certain rights in one U.S. tradition; "all men" are subject to corruption in Utopian definition, (so citizens do not do the butchering, representatives are not allowed to counsel in secret).

124. U.S. norms may be changing on this; whether the Mayday generation will continue past 30 in its enthusiasm for boat-rocking is, again, an interesting empirical question.

125. Studies of career choices of contemporary college graduates require some qualifications to this, although the scope of the shift is unclear. See Berger and Berger (1971).

126. The landmark work is Stouffer (1963). The simplest general definition, deviance as "difference from majority beliefs" (McCloskey and Schaar, 1965: 32-33), remphasizes the need for a way of precisely describing those beliefs.

127. The open term "awareness," usually narrowed to knowledge of particular aspects of the social or political system, does raise the interesting question of whether the model overpresumes; does it, like functionalism, impose upon the simpler organization a set of categories developed for and appropriate to the complex organization. In one aspect, this may be a valid criticism—that is, in reference to the appreciative system—that set of preferences concerning man, society, tradition, and the natural world. In a completely closed, ancient society with a single belief-value pattern, this in fact may be possible for a large majority of the populace. One may question, however, that mankind has ever been fully content with its lot—were it so, religion hardly would exist, and it is a common provider of that preferential system here postulated. The more particular issue is whether the simple model, which we have just suggested is not beyond the simple political man, has the capacity to deal with the broadly aware citizen of the modern communications-glutted world. To deal with this complexity, however, the model can be ramified to whatever extent necesary—e.g., beliefs about man_1, man_2, etc., for each category ego defines. Regarding available traditions, the modern, complex man may again have several definitional patterns and can be described in terms of that breadth; he can, for other analytic purposes, be "collapsed" into the summary categories of his (1) belief concerning the operable tradition and his (2) preference concerning some alternative.

128. Civic competence is defined by Matthews and Prothro as (1) the belief that public officials are influenced by ordinary citizens, (2) the knowledge about ways of influencing them, (3) sufficient self-confidence to attempt influence, when appropriate (scale reprinted in Robinson et al., 1968: 471-472). Political competence, as

defined in *The Civic Culture* (Almond and Verba, 1963), (scale reprinted an Robinson et al., 1968: 446-447) is similar in tapping both subjective and objective competence, but at the local level. Personal competence, as used in Survey Research Center polls (see Robinson et al., 1968: 655-660) is more general, involving the feeling that the respondent will be able to carry out his plans, has more good luck than bad, and some sureness about life. Political efficacy, first used in Campbell et al. (1954), and carried in recent SRC surveys, taps responsiveness of public offacials, comprehensibility of the governmental system, and the respondents' attitudes toward voting and the power of the vote. Participation, in Almond and Verba (1963: 169-179) involves knowledge about government input-output and the degree of obligation felt to participate in various levels of activity. Common also is a simple index based on voting, making campaign contributions, attending rallies, etc. (See Robinson et al., 1968: ch. 11.) The antithetical futility and impotence have been used extensively in McCloskey's PAB studies (e.g., McCloskey and Schaar, 1965). Cynicism we have covered above.

129. The type of association will depend on his third-dimension position: e.g., particularistic definition might direct him to church and fraternal organizations, universalistic definition to groups of greater heterogeneity.

130. The question of the group's responsiveness could be answered in terms of that group's modal definition of man, as well as the other dimensions. If, say, he fits their definition of man (a group of Calvinists might reject this particular individual as unduly cheerful), and is congruent in style and moral norms, then there would be a high probability of positive response, hypothetically.

131. This is a possible source of "parochials" in modern society; the term is that of Almond and Verba (1963: 17-19). The definition takes all its illustrations from nonmodern societies, although the "civic culture" does contain parochials (Almond and Verba, 1963: 31, 501).

132. See Chapter IV, Interpersonal Attitudes–ethnocentrism.

133. The definitions of futility and impotence follow this same mode of explication. The definition of cynicism is, in this *political* context, a rather simple application to the "beliefs concerning man" subsystem, where in some way the cognitions ego has of politicians fail to correspond to his preference, whatever that may be. Additionally, one hypothesizes a low tolerance for imperfection, an aspect of ego's moral norm position.

134. From the concepts used by Hegel and Marx (Marcuse, 1960: 246 and 273 ff.), to the simple "feeling of estrangement from one's peers" in Sniderman and Citrin (1971: 407).

135. See Seeman's 1959 classification listed in Miller (1970: 317).

136. Cf. Paul Bowles' novel, *The Sheltering Sky.*

137. This latter position is presumptively highly unstable; St Augustine comes to mind.

138. By "truly" we intend "congruence of cognition and preference."

139. E.g., Riesmann's "self-directed" (Riesmann, 1950) in distinction to his three imperfect types; or Fromm's mature personality (Fromm, 1955).

140. As *The Civic Culture* demonstrated, allegiance and its resultant patriotism need not be a function of allegiance "to a governmental system," but has many possible affect objects. See "System affect," (Almond and Verba, 1963: 102).

141. That the term "authoritarian" was a late substitution as noted in Christie (1954: 123-196, at 126).

142. As defined in Adorno et al. (1960: 228), the concept includes: conventionalism (see our discussion of rigidity), authoritarian submission (see dominance), authoritarian aggression (see aggression), anti-intraception (see, e.g., tough- tendermindedness), superstition (see mysticism) and stereotypy (see rigidity), power and toughness (see dominance, etc.), destruction and cynicism (see hostility, cynicism), projectivity and exaggerated concern with sex. The latter pair are related ("projectivity" is a "disposition to believe wild and dangerous things go on in the world," sex being one of them), and presently outside the model's competence. A similar index, used with disappointing results in the 1956 SRC postelection study (see Robinson et al., 1968: 654), includes attitudes concerning profession, the corrosive aspects of science, war as inevitable in human nature, and discipline. Cf. the "totalitarian" index (Sniderman and Citrin, 1971: 412): "Disregard for minorities, support for social change even if it requires ruthlessness, and intolerance of dissent."

143. A similar analysis may summarize the "Calvinist" or "Protestant ethic" orientation; see the discussion in Bendix (1962: 57ff.), from which the quotations are taken: Cognitive beliefs concerning man: complete discipline of the individual (aesceticism, "terrifying austerity"), rigorous self-orientation and extreme universalism; cognitive norms involve, according to the classic description, absolute belief, absolute self-validation (no one but the individual knows whether he is saved or damned), and universalistically defined "reality." (The real is utterly abstract, eliminating "all magical means of attaining salvation.") One might suggest additionally, following Fromm, that there is here no preferential system the existence of which would probably vary,—given the rigor of the cognitive system—and thus represent revolt against the deity. The eujorative concept of "responsibility," related to ego strength (McCloskey, 1967: 72), is oddly similar: self-definition in terms of discipline, usually other-oriented, with further definition according to the focus of responsibility: particularism or universalism.

144. Rather, that is, than attempting to force rough-edged reality into a single mold, as too frequently is done.

145. Semantic complexities aside, left is commonly associated with "liberalism," right with "conservatism." See, for the everyday view, Plano and Greenberg (1962: 9, 14). Illustrative indices are found in Sniderman and Citrin (1971: 411-412): "right wing" is defined as agreement with statements against liberals, do-gooders and left wingers, fear for the American way of life and for freedom and initiative; "left wing" is defined as agreement ith statements favoring socialist economic principles, attacking American society as controlled by the wealthy, and as not a free society. The liberalism-conservatism indices are summarized and evaluated in Robinson et al. (1968: 79-160). It is interesting to note that in the cases studying left vs. right and liberal vs. conservative, the results suggest that there is not in fact a continuum but rather that there are separate factors.

146. As a severe departure from the established pattern (and even then subjective determinations will vary).

147. The semantic difficulties involved with the individual who seeks to maximize moderation will not be considered at this point.

148. Distinctions in patterns of so-called "radical" behavior can be made similarly.

149. See discussion of Calvinism below.

150. The "direct action" index (see Sniderman and Citrin, 1971: 411-412) relates to extremist political behavior, but also plausibly to the efficient administra-

tor who cuts "red tape," and who would be defined *in vacuo* as a combination of cognitive norms: skepticism of established (traditional) practices; and self-orientation, leading the individual to "take responsibility," or "to take matters into his own hands." The third dimension here would define the type of behavior—one may start a revolution because the immediate situation is real and intolerable, or because one sees the shadow of the *Weltgeist*. The reasons conducive to such attitudes and subsequent behavior would be explicated by facets of the model already dealt with (see, e.g., alienation).

151. Gratifying, or not; self- or other-oriented, etc.

152. An additional factor in producing extremists is suggested by Sniderman and Citrin's summary definition (1971: 410-411) as a "general preference for simple explanations and solutions." A cognitive component can thus be brought in, using the third dimension of that mode—a particularistic orientation to the immediate, in lieu of more complex theoretic explanations. There are of course other possibilities.

153. This dimension of political orientation may be traced as far back as Socrates and Plato; for contemporary usage see *supra* note 96.

154. Let us say, for instance, that an individual believes (cognitively) that men are in fact equal (by nature, as it were), yet perceives society's definition to be particularistic, based on wealth or religion or race or other such criteria. If he is among the favored classes, one might expect his egalitarianism to surface as some of those attitudes generally called liberalism, or if he is a maximizer, as a revolutionary of the Kropotkin type. On the other hand, an individual with the same attitudes but a member of an unfavored grouping within the society probably will mean by "equality" a new (particularistic) inequality, but one that places him at the top.

155. A variety of remaining concepts involve almost solely the individual's definition of the political object world and his relation to it. The "independence of government" index (Sniderman and Citrin, 1971: 410) involves a consistent self-orientation, which remains uninvolved with government under all circumstances ("I'd rather starve. . . ."). Formally equivalent at this particular point in the model would be the *traditional* or *subject* (Almond and Verba, 1963) individual, who for other reasons is not included within any or some of the aspects of the political system. Another definitional dichotomy—localism vs. cosmopolitanism—similarly is a question of whether various political systems are defined as including the individual. (Dye, 1966: 239-246; see Robinson et al., 1968: 397-346, 400-405). This, as in the case of ethnocentrism, would at the level of individual analysis produce attention ranges of various complexity; that positions on this dimension tend to correlate with other issue positions may be useful in developing the chronological outcomes of various pattern modes. Finally, one may mention two tangential but interesting concepts—nostalgia and identification with the underdog (see, respectively, the Survey Research Center items listed in Robinson et al., 1968: 653, 663; and Schuman and Harding's 1963 scale in Robinson et al., 1968: 223-229). The former may be seen as a function of adherence to an early belief pattern, followed by a change in the social or environmental situation which leaves the individual isolated in an "out of date" belief pattern; this commonly produces a sense that "you can't lead a truly moral life these days" and correlates with broader political syndromes. Sympathy with the underdog presumably first requires that in some way the ego involved has felt himself to *be* an underdog—excessive discipline from authorities that reject him from inclusion might be one genesis. "Sympathy" would be a response to other persons perceived to be "like" one's self; exactly why it results—rather than aggression—possibly may be conceptualized in terms of the self-other distinction.

156. It was the original intent here to investigate the model's utility in the development of empirically useful typologies by converting to the model's concepts the "types of men" explicated by Spranger and used by, among others, Lasswell and the Allport-Vernon value studies. This, however, would have required use of the model's full range of subsystems to adequately describe Spranger's "ideal" six types, as well as the important subtypes and cross-types; such analysis seemed premature. See Spranger (1966), Allport and Vernon (1931); for Lasswell's theoretical discussions of types see Lasswell (1962) esp. ch. IV "Varieties of Character and Personality"; the present approach is closer to his well-known value list, (Lasswell, 1962: 17), and "The Selective Effect of Personality on Political Participation" (Christie and Jahoda, 1954: 197-225).

157. There seems an implicit agreement that 'rationality', while an extremely complex problem, can be considered only in terms of means used, not goals; cf. Downs (1957: 5): ". . . the term rational is never applied to an agent's ends, but only to his means." What the present typology intends is the addition of at least partial conceptual clarity to this unexamined theoretical opportunity for additional goal patterns.

158. Spranger (1966: 174ff.) suggests these and other affinities and antipathies.

159. Religious man, e.g., is not considered in a religious context; though there is no barrier to analyzing religious phenomena from a political aspect.

160. Classic utilizations of the economic approach to man are Buchanan and Tullock (1962), and Downs (1957); Spranger (1966: 130-146) discusses "The Economic Attitude."

161. Rousseau's discussion of the man who "took it into his head to say *this is mine* and found people simple enough to believe him" is in Part II of the Discourse on Inequality (Masters, 1964: 141). That man's impulse to say "this is my own" is the basis of the state (indeed of virtue itself) is defended in Aristotle's *Politics*, Book II, chs. 305 (Sinclair, 1962: 58-59).

162. While this discussion may seem to raise deeper problems of rationality, it does not add materially to the confusion already implicit in use of the term. Economic Man, as Spranger suggests, *is* interested in causality, but only insofar as it is immediately evident and useful. That he is, therefore, both scientific and *a*theoretic may appear inconsistent; the combination is not however unknown empirically.

163. This description owes much to Spranger's discussion (1966: 130-146).

164. This sort of distinction might prove useful in clarifying the difficulty often encountered by students of Hobbes: that given the nature of man as he describes it, ". . . nothing but the strongest of powers can maintain society in being" (Jouvenel, 1957: 246). To the contrary, we would suggest that self-interested man, if he has the taste for *abstract* definition leading to *long-range interpretations* of that self-interest, under stable circumstances, could become civil without any need for a coercive Leviathan. Morton Kaplan's (1957: 50-52) adoption of Hobbes in his definition of the "unit veto" international system is relevant to this point. Beliefs concerning the object world, for at least the "Western" variety of Economic Man may be sketched in to suggest the model's capacity to cope with apparently inconsistent attitudes. Spranger, in his description of the economic type, notes that while the type is interested in causal relations and is thus scientific in that sense, it also believes in luck. With the cognitive aspect covered earlier, the question of luck is defined in the current module: a particularistic pattern of expectations concerning the "universe"

and its gifts. Once again this raises some possible analogies with cultures characterized by nonlogical orientations.

165. Since he may be an atheist, the title used here may be unfortunate; it is used by Spranger, is implicit in many studies of the genre, and is no more misleading than alternative terms. (Chiliastic man has been suggested; this is substantively accurate.)

166. Hoffer (1951: 10); Hoffer also emphasizes (1951: 60 ff.) two of our defining characteristics—self-sacrifice and identification with a collective whole.

167. Proudhon's response to Marx in 1846 makes the distinction clear; he defends the workers from charges of ideological impurity on the grounds that after all "We must live, that is to say, buy bread, fuel, meat, and we must pay our rent" (Edwards, 1969: 153).

168. The cognitive aspect of "other" validation seems necessary to create true extremism; if the individual is a self-validator (and believer) he may simply "drop out" of an unsatisfying situation; this is not a *directly* political outcome.

169. The "selfish" aspect of Principled Man should cause protest. The principles he uses may socially benefit others; may have been in fact initially developed (in, say, some ethical system) for that purpose. Principled man, having internalized the norms (see, e.g., Riesmann's inner-directed type) uses them however for his own satisfaction. The attitude shows in the motto *fiat justitia, ruat caelum:* the *principle* here is clearly favored over any of its *consequences.*

170. Were the second dimension to emphasize self, one would have the independent *creator* of moral systems, or the theorist. See Spranger (1966: 109-129), on the theoretic attitude." That we here pass by this extremely interesting type is again a function of our focus on the political arena (rather than attempting to encompass all human activity).

171. It may be argued that these types are merely Economic Men guided by long-run (and thus somewhat obscured) self-interest. This seems unlikely: the opening sections of Plato's Republic are evidence enough that mankind long has been aware virtue was not likely to be rewarded; nor have current investigations of decision-making under uncertainty given any greater grounds for such a possibility.

172. And, of course, on theoretical ones: in terms of moral norms the power orientation is defined as a principled type on the basis of its abstract, nonparticularistic goals.

REFERENCES

ABELSON, R. P., and CARROLL, J. D. (1965) "Computer simulation of individual belief systems" Amer. Behav. Scientist 8: 24-30.

ADORNO, T. W. (1950) The Authoritarian Personality. New York: Harper Brothers.

ALKER, H. R., Jr. (1965) Mathematics and Politics. New York: Macmillan.

ALLPORT, G. W. and P. E. VERNON (1931) A Study of Values. Boston: Houghton Mifflin.

ALMOND, G. and S. VERBA (1963) The Civic Culture. Princeton: Princeton Univ. Press.

BARRON, F. (1953) "An Ego-strength scale which predicts response to psychotherapy." J. of Consult. Psych. 17: 327-333.

BENDIX, R. (1962) Max Weber: An Intellectual Portrait. Garden City: Anchor.

BERGER, P. L. and B. BERGER (1971) "Youth 'greening' may turn blue." Washington Post.

BERKOWITZ, L. (1968) "Social motivation," p. 52 in G. Lindzey and E. Aronson (eds.) Handbook of Social Psychology. Reading: Mass. Addison Wesley.

BLACK, G. S. (1972) "A theory of political ambition: career choices and the role of structural incentives." Amer. Pol. Sci. Rev. 66: 1 (March): 144-159.

BONJEAN, C., R. HILL, and D. MCLEMORE (1967) Sociological Measurement: An Inventory of Scales and Indices. San Francisco: Chandler.

BOORSTIN, D. J. (1953) The Genius of American Politics. Chicago: Phoenix.

BORGATTA, E. J. and W. W. LAMBERT [eds.] (1968) Handbook of Personality Theory and Research. Chicago: Rand McNally.

BOWLES, P. (1968) Sheltering Sky. New York: New Directions.

BRIM, O. G., Jr. (1968) "Adult socialization," pp. 182-226 in J. A. Clausen (ed.) Socialization and Society. Boston: Little, Brown.

BUCHANAN, J. and G. TULLOCK (1962) The Calculus of Consent. Ann Arbor: Univ. of Michigan Press.

CAMPBELL, D. (1958) "Common fate, similarity and other indices of the status of aggregates of persons as social entities." Behavioral Sci. 3: 14-25.

CAMPBELL, A., P. E. CONVERSE, W. E. MILLER, and D. E. STOKES (1964) The American Voter: An Abridgement. New York: John Wiley.

――― G. GURIN and W. E. MILLER (1954) The Voter Decides. Evanston: Row, Peterson.

CATTELL, R. B. (1946) Description and Measurement of Personality. Yonkers: Worldbook Company.

CHRISTIE, R. and M. JAHODA [eds.] (1954) Studies in the Scope and Method of "The Authoritarian Personality." Glencoe: Free Press.

CHRISTIE, R. (1954) "Authoritarianism re-examined," pp. 123-196 in R. Christie and M. Jahoda (eds.) Studies in the Scope and Method of "The Authoritarian Personality." Glencoe: Free Press.

CLAUSEN, J. A. (1968) Socialization and Society. Boston: Little, Brown.

COPLESTON, F. (1963) A History of Philosophy: Volume 3: 11. New York: Image.

DAHL, R. A. (1963) Modern Political Analysis. Englewood Cliffs, N.J.: Prentice-Hall.

――― (1956) Preface to Democratic Theory. Chicago: Univ. of Chicago Press.

DAHRENDORF, R. (1968) Essays in the Theory of Society. Stanford: Stanford Univ. Press.

DEUTSCH, K. (1963) The Nerves of Government: Models of Political Communication and Control. New York: Free Press.

DOWNS, A. (1957) An Economic Theory of Democracy. New York: Harper & Row.

DOSTOEVSKI, F. (1957) The Brothers Karamazov. New York: Signet.

DUBIN, R. (1960) "Parsons' actor: continuities in social theory." Amer. Soc. Rev. 25: 4 (August): 457-466.

DYE, T. R. (1966) "The localism-cosmopolitan dimension and the study of urban politics." Social Forces 41: 239-246.

EASTON, D. (1965) A Systems Analysis of Political Life. New York: John Wiley.

EDWARDS, S. [ed.] (1969) Selected Writings of P. -J. Proudhon. Garden City: Anchor.

EISENBERG, L. (1972) "The human nature of human nature." Science (April): 123-128.

[68]

EYSENCK, H. J. (1953) Structure of Human Personality. New York: John Wiley.
FESTINGER, L. (1957) A Theory of Cognitive Dissonance. Evanston: Row, Peterson.
FRENKEL-BRUNSWIK, E. (1949a) "A study of prejudice in children." Human Relations 1: 295-306.
--- (1949b) "Intolerance of ambiguity as an emotional personality variable." J. of Personality 18: 108-143.
FROMM, E. (1955) The Sane Society. Greenwich: Fawcett.
--- (1941) Escape From Freedom. New York: Avon.
GREENSTEIN, F. I. (1969) Personality and Politics: Problems of Evidence, Inference and Conceptualization. Chicago: Markham.
HELMBOLD, W. C. [trans.] (1952) Gorgias: Plato. Indianapolis: Bobbs-Merrill.
HOBBES, T. (1958) Leviathan. Indianapolis: Bobbs-Merril.
HOFFER, E. (1951) The True Believer. New York: Harper & Brothers.
HOMANS, G. C. (1950) The Human Group. New York: Harcourt Brace and Company.
HOROWITZ, I. L. [ed.] (1967) The Rise and Fall of Project Camelot. Cambridge: MIT Press.
HSU, F.L.K. [ed.] (1961) Psychological Anthropology: Approaches to Culture and Personality. Homewood, Ill.: Dorsey.
HUME, D. (1961) A Treatise of Human Nature. Garden City: Dolphin.
JOUVENEL, B. D. (1963) The Pure Theory of Politics. New Haven: Yale Univ. Press.
--- (1957) Sovereignty. Chicago: University of Chicago-Phoenix.
JOWETT, B. [trans.] (1942) Five Dialogs. New York: Van Nostrand.
KAPLAN, A. (1964) Conduct of Inquiry. San Francisco: Chandler.
KAPLAN, B. [ed.] (1961) Studying Personality Cross-Culturally. Evanston: Row, Peterson.
KAPLAN, M. (1957) System and Process in International Politics. New York: John Wiley.
KLAUSNER, S. Z. [ed.] (1967) The Study of Total Societies. Garden City: Doubleday Anchor.
KLUCKHOHN, C. (1951) "Value and value-orientations in the theory of action: an exploration in definition and classification," pp. 388-433 in T. Parsons and E. A. Shils (eds.) Toward a General Theory of Action: Theoretical Foundations for the Social Sciences. Cambridge: Harvard Univ. Press.
KUHN, T. S. (1962) The Structure of Scientific Revolutions. Chicago: Phoenix.
LAING, R. D. and A. ESTERSON (1970) Sanity, Madness and the Family. Baltimore: Pelican.
LANDAU, M. (1972) Political Theory and Political Science. New York: Macmillan.
LANE, R. E. (1969) Political Thinking and Consciousness. Chicago: Markham.
--- (1962) Political Ideology. New York: Free Press.
LERNER, M. (1969) "Bibliographic note," pp. 154-184 in F. I. Greenstein (ed.) Personality and Politics: Problems of Evidence, Inference and Conceptualization. Chicago: Markham.
--- (1940) The Prince and the Discourses. New York: Modern Library.
LASSWELL, H. D. (1962) Power and Personality. New York: Viking.
--- (1954) "The selective effect of personality on political participation," pp. 197-225 in R. Christie and M. Jahoda (eds.) Studies in the Scope and Method of "The Authoritarian Personality." Glencoe: Free Press.

––– and A. KAPLAN (1950) Power and Society: A Framework for Political Inquiry. New Haven: Yale Univ. Press.

LEVI-STRAUSS, C. (1967) Structural Anthropology. Garden City: Doubleday.

––– (1966) The Savage Mind. Chicago: Univ. of Chicago Press.

––– (1963) Totemism. Boston: Beacon.

LINDZEY, G. and E. ARONSON [eds.] (1968) Handbook of Social Psychology. Reading, Mass.: Addison Wesley.

LIJPHART, A. (1971) "Comparative Politics and the comparative method." Amer. Pol. Sci. Rev. 55: 3 (September): 682-693.

LOEHLIN, J. C. (1968) Computer Models of Personality. New York: Random House.

LORENZ, K. (1966) On Aggression. New York: Bantam.

McCLOSKEY, H. (1967) "Personality and attitude correlates of foreign policy orientations," p. 71 in J. N. Rosenau Domestic Sources of Foreign Policy. New York: Free Press.

––– and J. H. SCHAAR (1965) "Psychological dimensions of anomy." Amer. Soc. Rev. 30: 1 (Feburary): 14-40.

McGUIRE, W. J. (1968) "The nature of attitudes and attitude change," pp. 136-314 in G. Lindzey and E. Aronson (eds.) Handbook of Social Psychology. Reading, Mass.: Addison Wesley.

McKINNEY, J. C. (1966) Constructive Typology and Social Theory. New York: Appleton-Century-Crofts.

MACRIDIS, R. (1955) The Study of Comparative Government. New York: Random House.

MANNHEIM, K. (n.d.) Ideology and Utopia. New York: Harcourt, Brace and World.

MARCUSE, H. (1960) Reason and Revolution. Boston: Beacon.

MARLOWE, D. and K. J. GERGEN (1968) "Personality and social interaction," pp. 590-665 in G. Lindzey and E. Aronson (eds.) Handbook of Social Psychology. Reading, Mass.: Addison Wesley.

MASON, P. (1970) Patterns of Dominance. London: Oxford Univ. Press.

MASTERS, R. D. [ed.] (1964) The First and Second Discourses. New York: St. Martin's press.

MEEHAN, E. (1967) Contemporary Political Thought. A Critical Study. Homewood, Ill.: Dorsey Press.

MILLER, D. C. (1970) Handbook of Research Design and Social Measurement. New York: David McKay.

MORE, T. (1964) Utopia. New Haven: Yale Univ. Press.

MURRAY, H. (1938) Explorations in Personality. New York: Oxford Univ. Press.

NIETZSCHE, F. (1961) Thus Spake Zarathustra. Baltimore: Penguin.

NORTHROP, F.S.C. (1960) Philosophical Anthropology and Practical Politics. New York: Macmillan.

PALMA, G. D. and H. McCLOSKEY (1970) "Personality and conformity: the learning of political attitudes." Amer. Pol. Sci. Rev. 54: 4 (December): 1054-1073.

PARSONS, T. (1960) "Pattern variables revisited: a response to Robert Dubin." Amer. Soc. Rev. 25: 4 (August): 467-483.

––– (1951) The Social System. Glencoe: Free Press.

––– and E. A. SHILS [eds.] (1951) Toward a General Theory of Action: Theoretical Foundations for the Social Sciences. Cambridge: Harvard Univ. Press.

PLANO, J. and M. GREENBERG (1962) The American Political Dictionary. New York: Holt, Rinehart & Winston.

PYE, L. W. and S. VERBA [eds.] (1965) Political Culture and Political Development. Princeton: Princeton Univ. Press.

RAPOPORT, A. (1966) "Some system approaches to political theory," p. 129 in D. Easton (ed.) Varieties of Political Theory. Englewood Cliffs, N.J.: Prentice-Hall.

– – – (1953) Operational Philosophy: Integrating Knowledge and Action. New York: Harper and Brothers.

RIESMANN, D. (1950) The Lonely Crowd. New Haven: Yale Univ. Press.

ROBINSON, J. P. and P. R. SHAVER (1969) Handbook of Research Design and Social Measurement. New York: David McKay.

– – – J. G. RUSK, and K. B. HEAD (1968) Measures of Political Attitudes. Ann Arbor: Institute for Social Research.

ROKEACH, M. (1968) Beliefs, Attitudes and Values. San Francisco: Jossey-Bass.

– – – (1960) The Open and Closed Mind: Investigations into the Nature of Belief Systems and Personality Systems. New York: Basic Books.

RUSSELL, B. (1945) A History of Western Philosophy. New York: Simon & Schuster.

SABINE, G. (1937) A History of Political Theory. New York: Henry Holt.

SARTORI, G. (1970) "Concept misformation in comparative politics." Amer. Pol. Sci. Rev. 54: 4 (December): 1033-1053.

– – – (1969) "From the Sociology of Politics to Political Sociology," pp. 65-100 in S. M. Lipset (ed.) Politics and the Social Sciences. New York: Oxford Univ. Press.

SHAW, M. and J. WRIGHT (1967) Scales for the Measurement of Attitudes. New York: McGraw Hill.

SHUBIK, M. (1964) Game Theory and Related Approaches to Social Behavior: Selections. New York: John Wiley.

SIGEL, R. (1970) Learning About Politics. New York: Random House.

SINCLAIR, J. A. [trans.] (1962) The Politics. New York: Penguin.

SNIDERMAN, P. M. and J. CITRIN (1971) "Psychological sources of political belief: self-esteem and isolationist attitudes." Amer. Pol. Sci. Rev. 55: 2 (June): 407.

SPRANGER, E. (1966) Types of Men: Psychology and Ethics of Personality. New York: Johnson Reprint Corporation.

STINCHCOMBE, A. L. (1968) Constructing Social Theories. New York: Harcourt, Brace and World.

STOUFFER, S. (1963) Communism, Conformism and Civil Liberties. Gloucester: Peter Smith.

TAYLOR, A. E. [trans.] (1960) Plato: The Laws. London: Dent.

THOMAS, W. I. and F. ZNANIECKI (1965) "Three types of personality," pp. 934-935 in T. Parsons (ed.) Theories of Society. New York: Free Press.

VERBA, S. (1965) "Comparative political culture," pp. 512-560 in L. W. Pye and S. Verba (eds.) Political Culture and Political Development. Princeton: Princeton Univ. Press.

VAN NEUMANN, J. (1958) The Computer and the Brain. New Haven: Yale Univ. Press.

WIENER, N. (1948) Cybernetics. Cambridge: MIT Press.

WOODGER, J. H. (1939) "The technique of theory construction." International Encyclopedia of Unified Science II: 5: 75.

YOUNG, O. (1968) Systems of Political Science. Englewood Cliffs, N.J.: Prentice-Hall.

ZIGLER, E. and I. L. CHILD (1968) "Socialization," pp. 450-589 in G. Lindzey and E. Aronson (eds.) Handbook of Social Psychology. Reading, Mass. Addison Wesley.

RUTH LANE is presently Assistant Professor of Political Science in the School of Government and Public Administration at The American University. Dr. Lane received her Ph.D. from Georgetown University; her dissertation was entitled, "A Computer Simulation of Voting in the U.S. House of Representatives." Since 1968, she has been engaged in teaching political methodology and traditional political theory.